I0491845

THANK YOU FOR YOUR PURCHASE

I hope you enjoy this coloring book.
May in bring you peace and relaxation.
To find other great products
visit TerryHelliker.com.

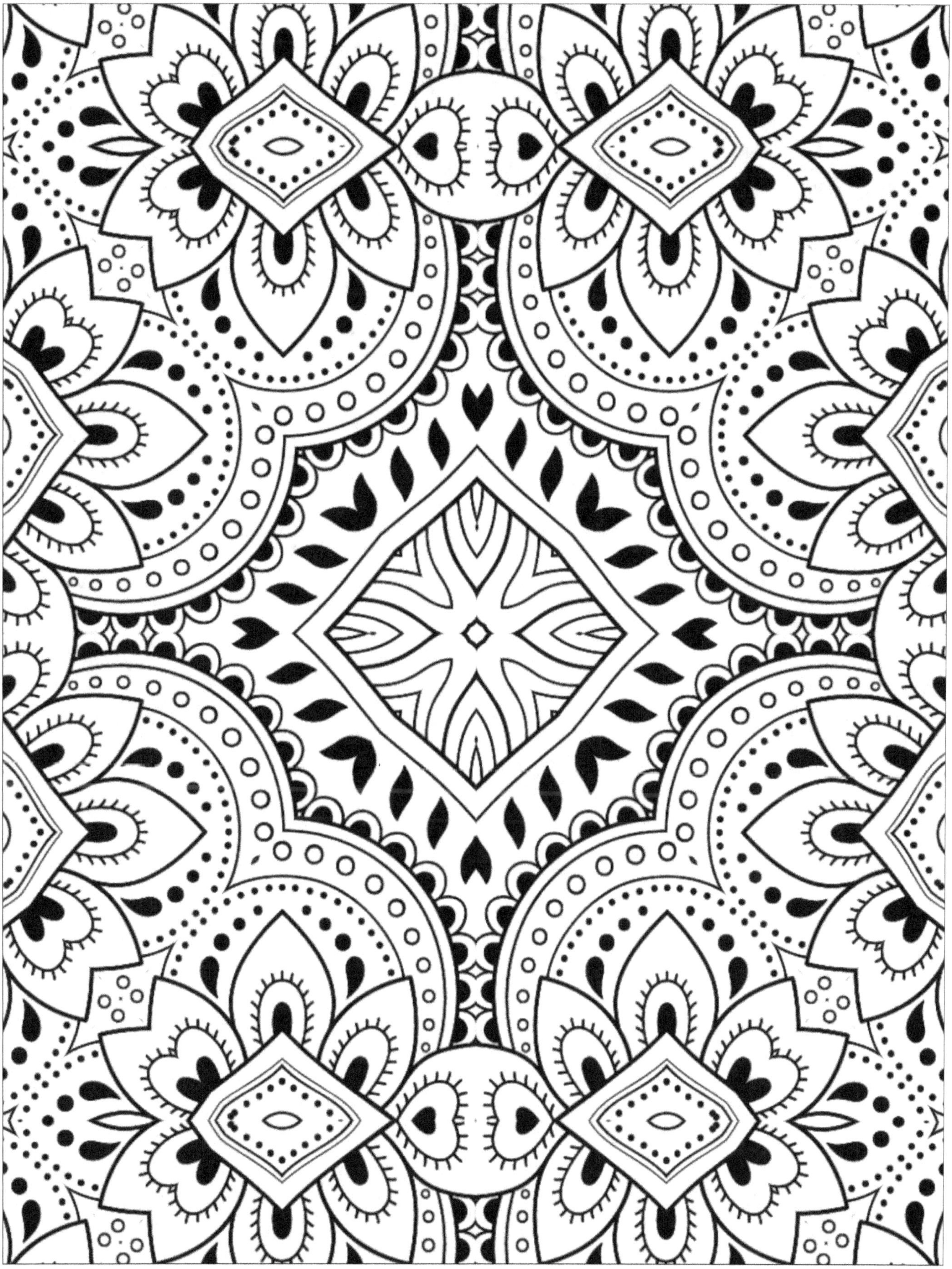

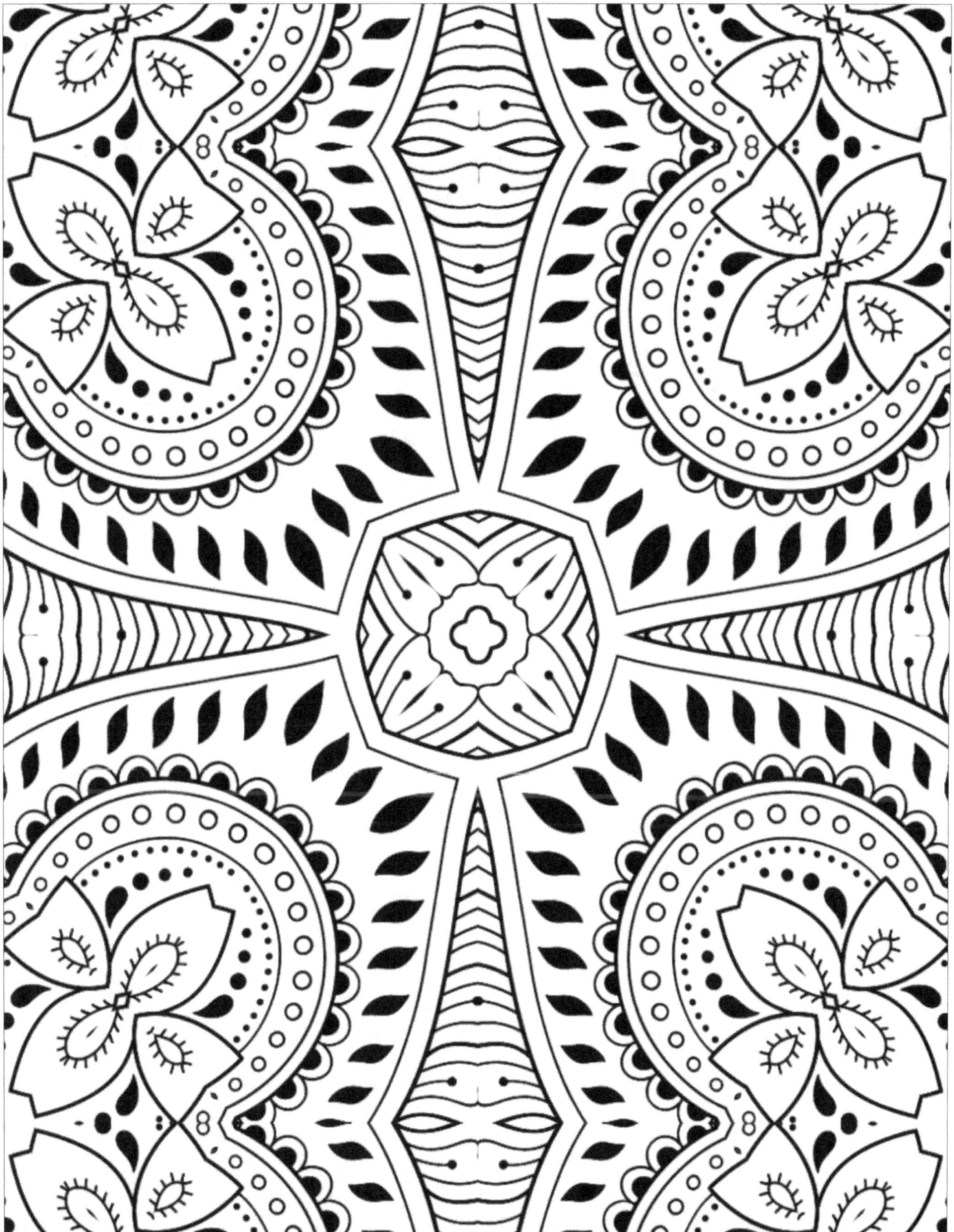

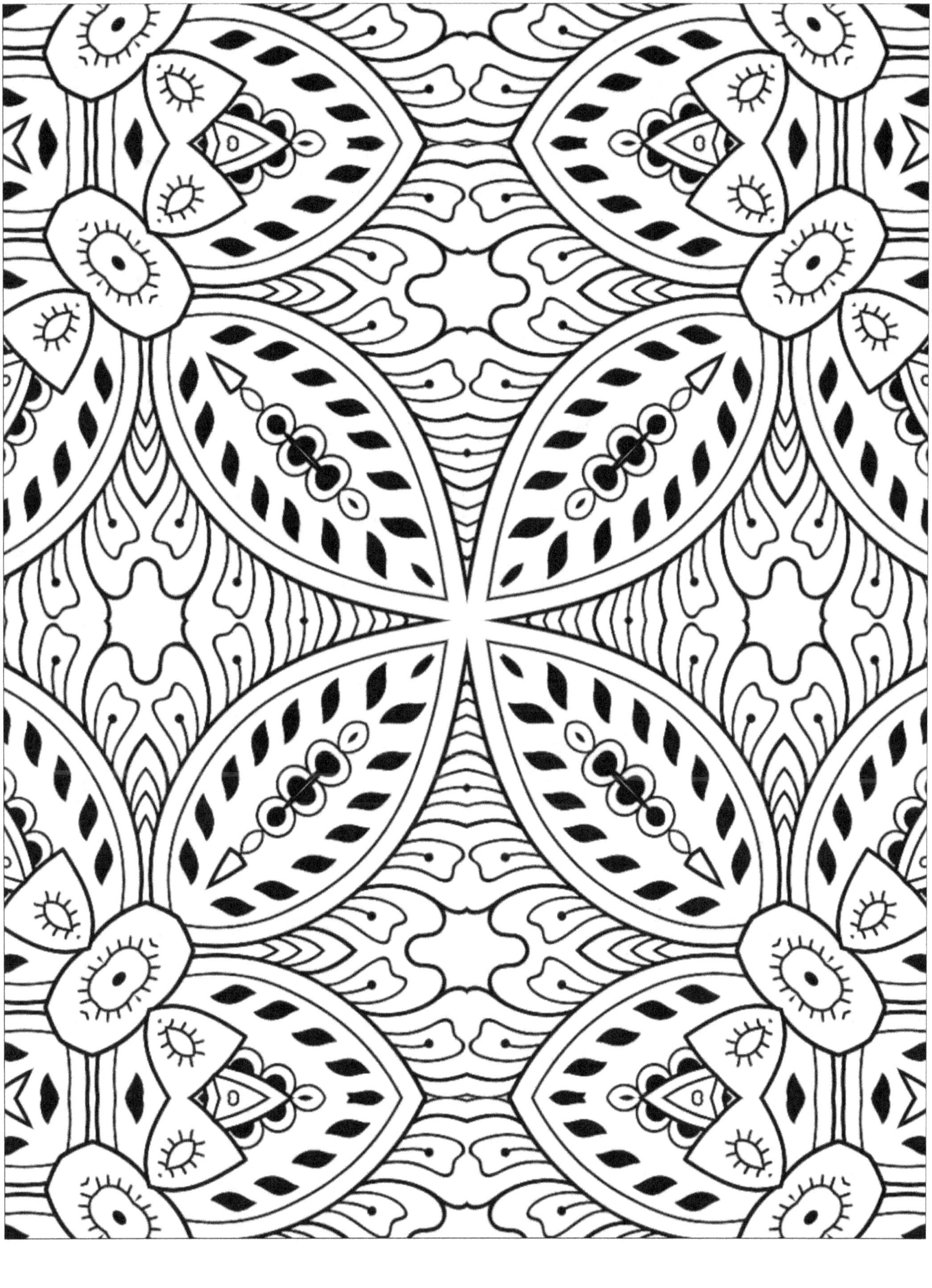

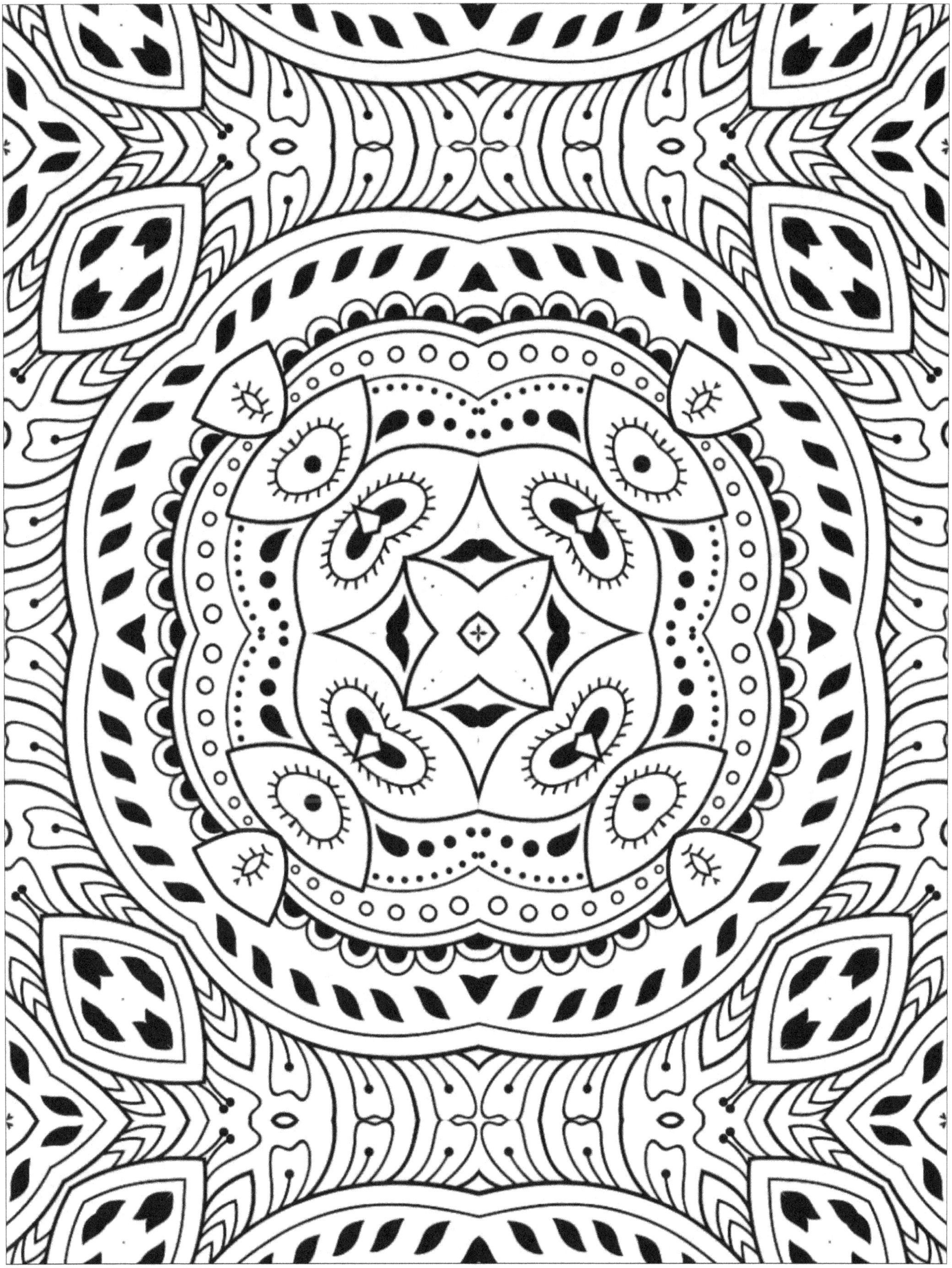

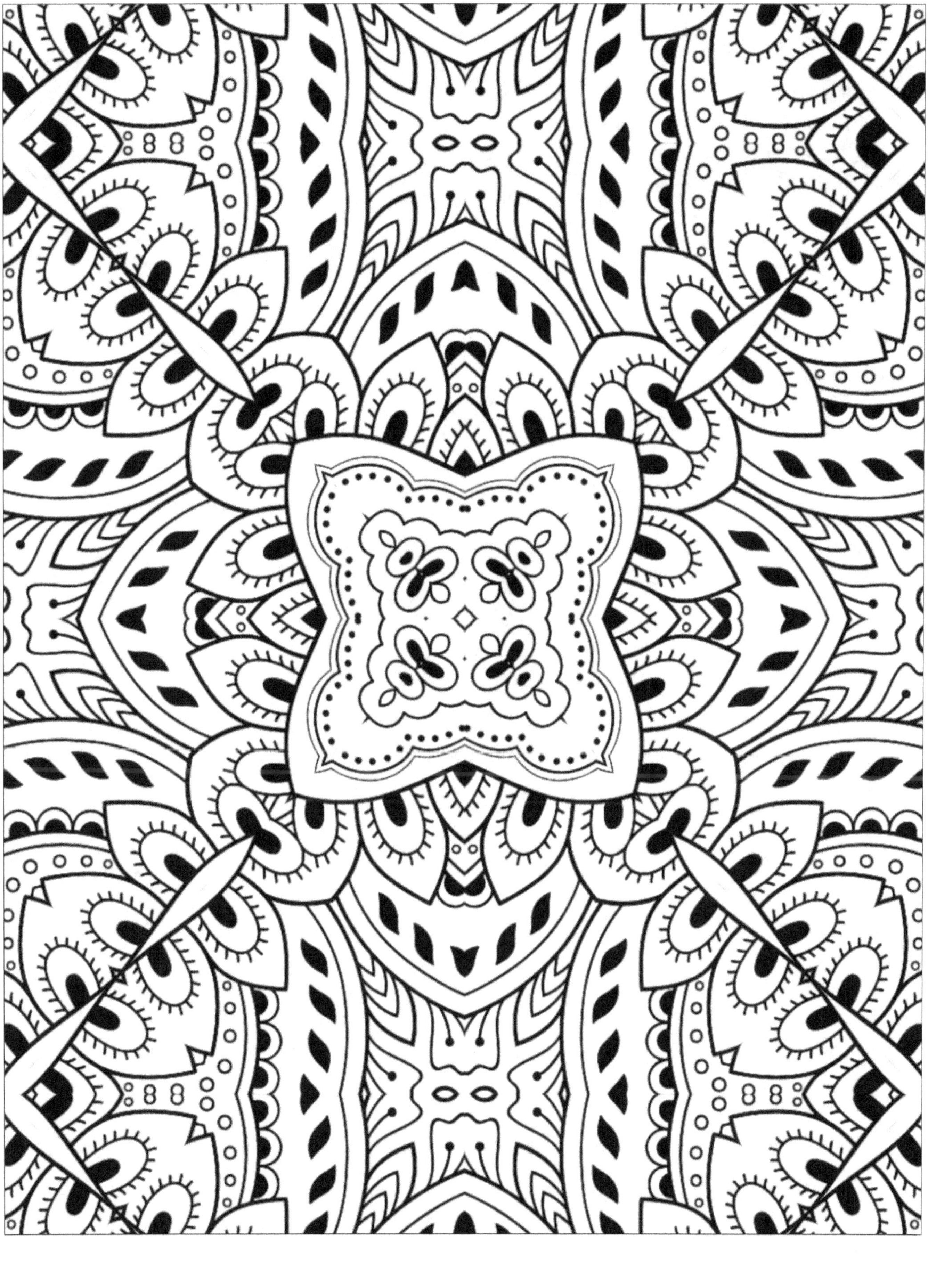

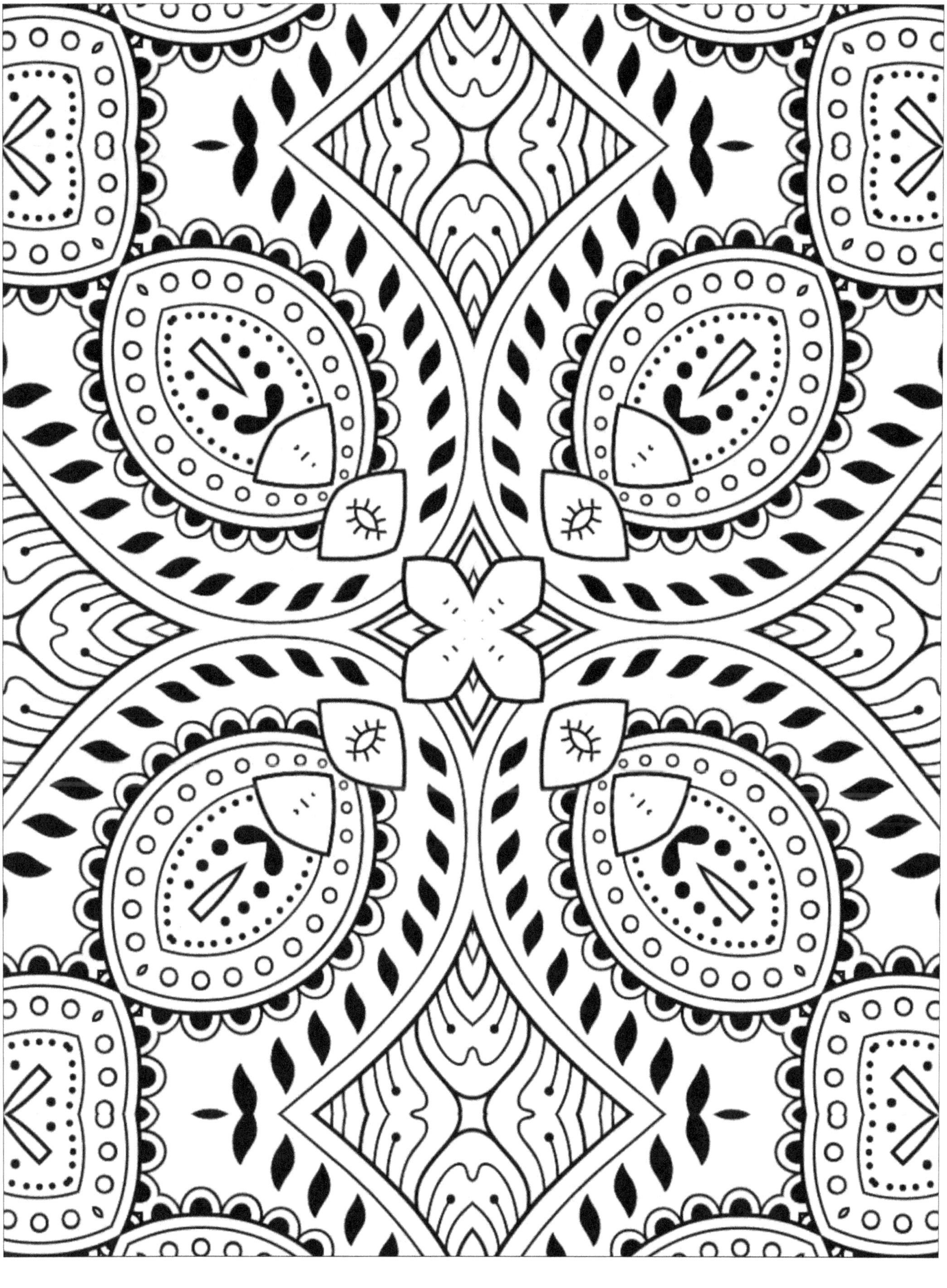

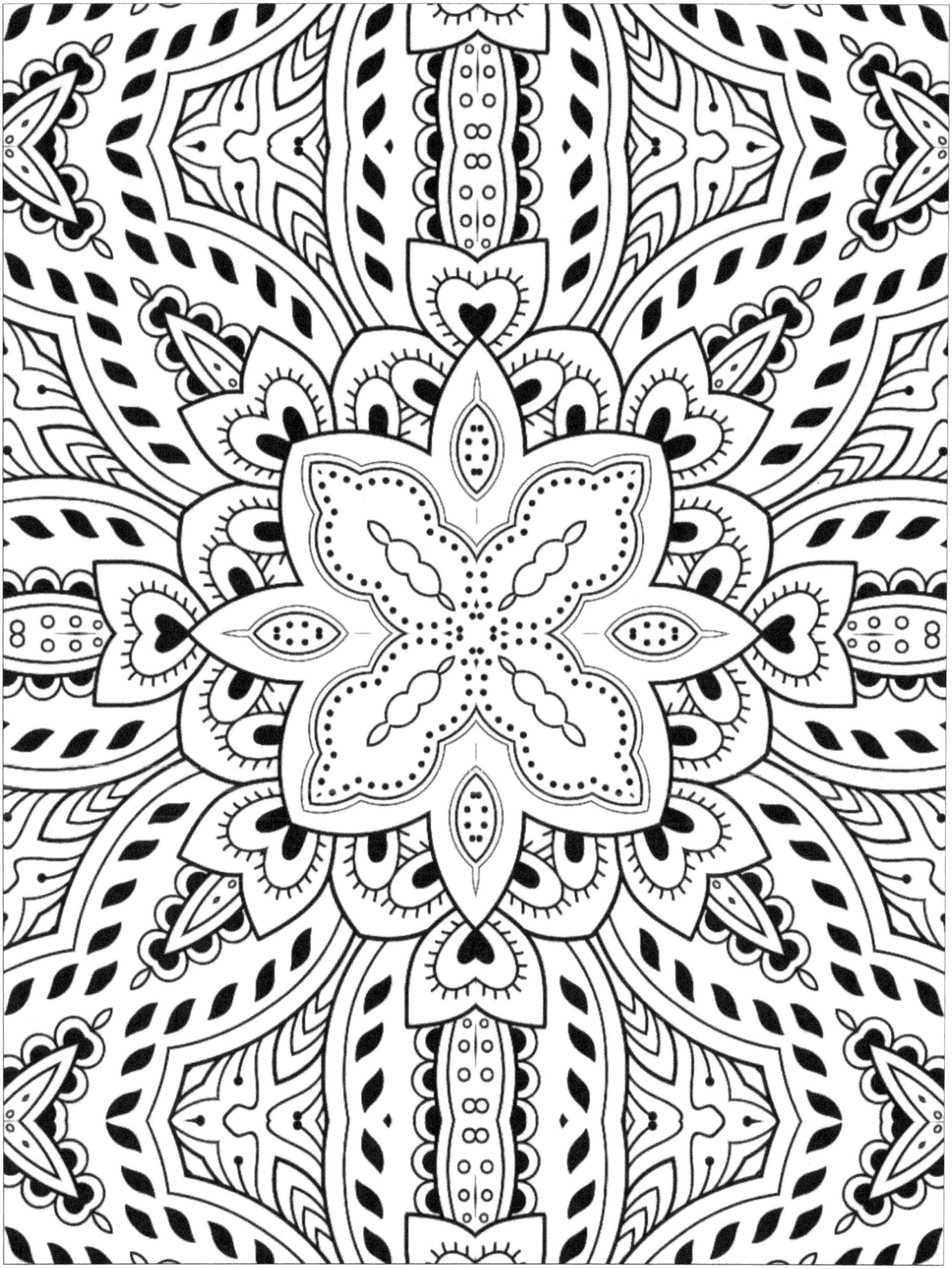

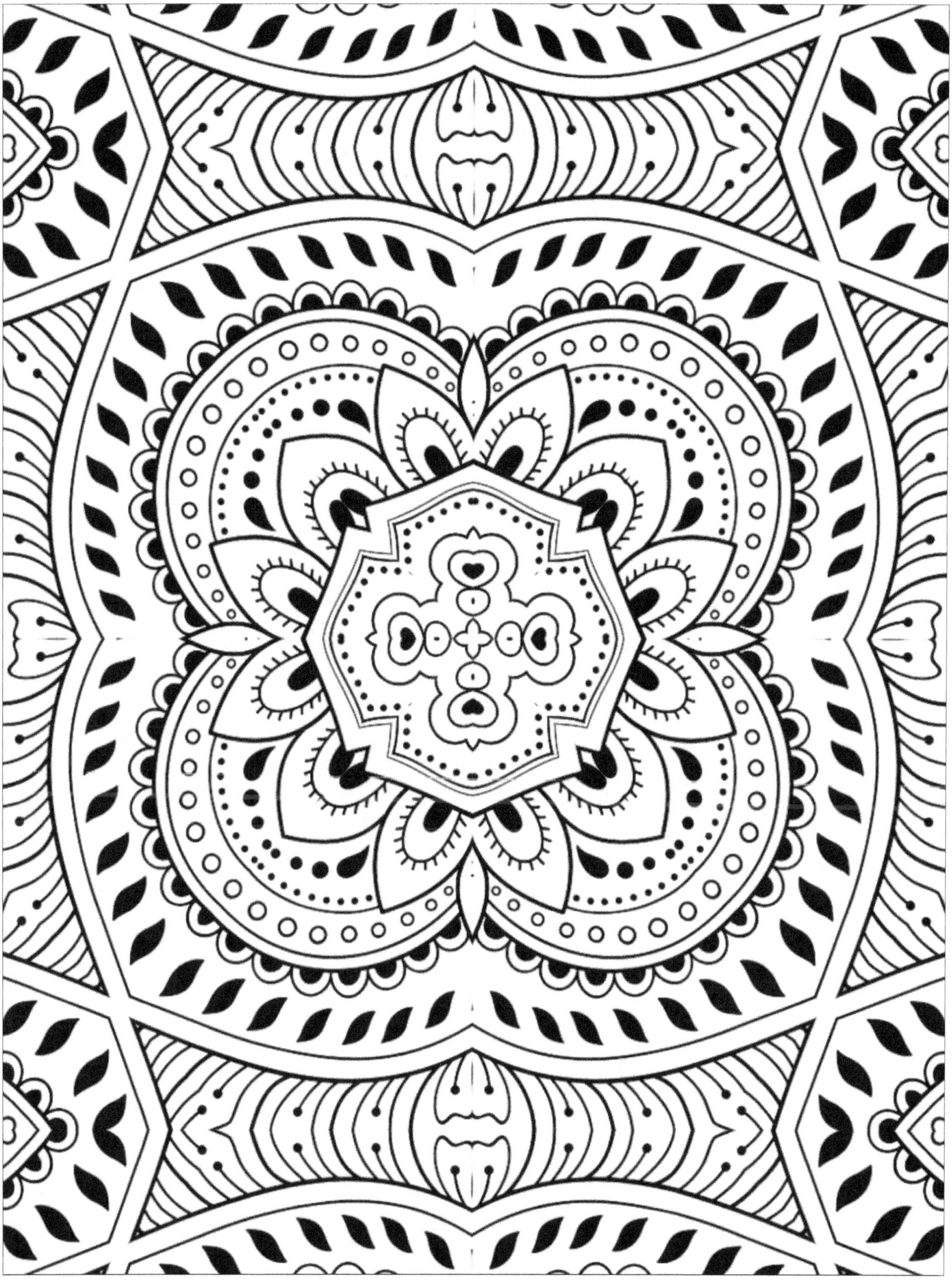

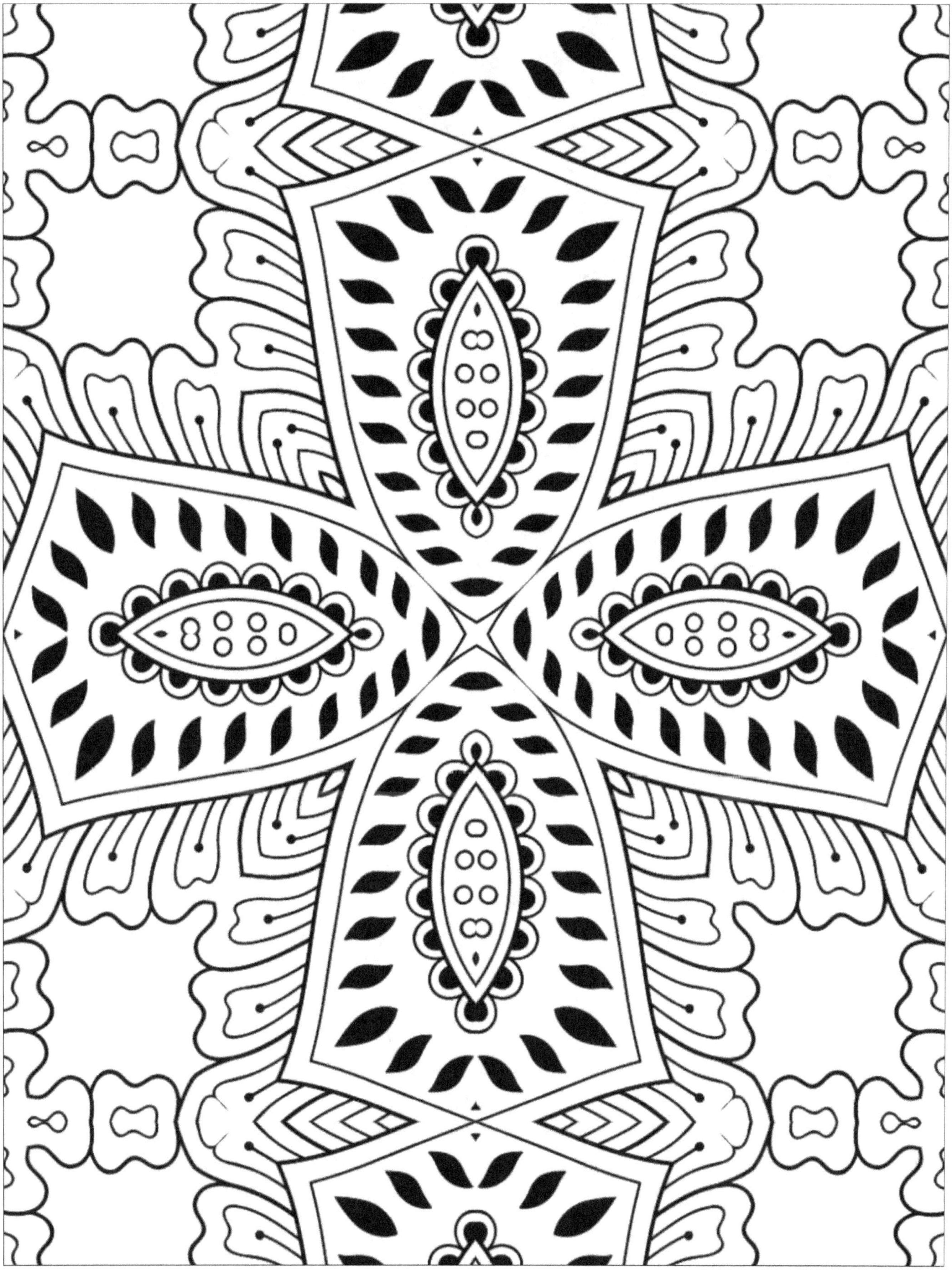

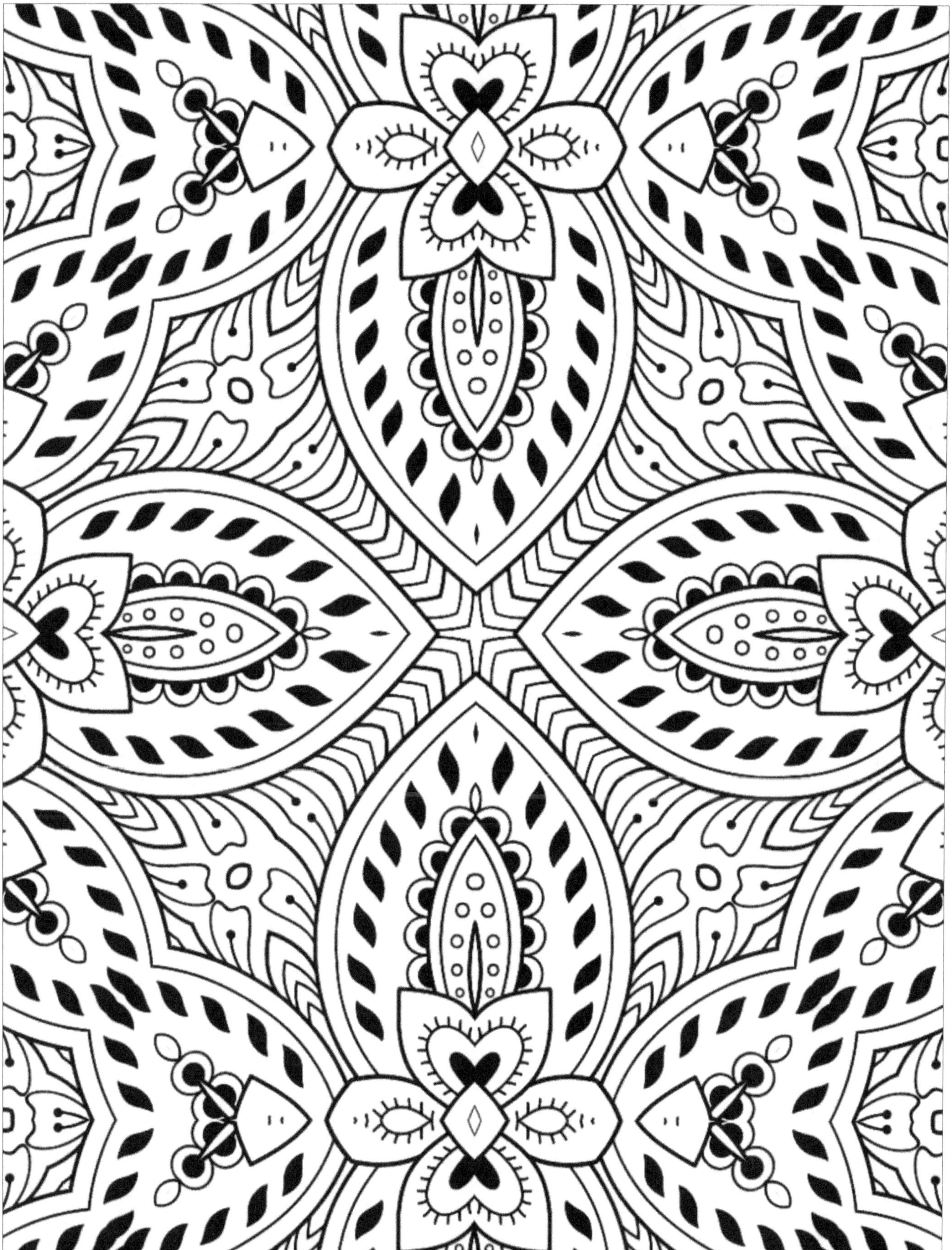

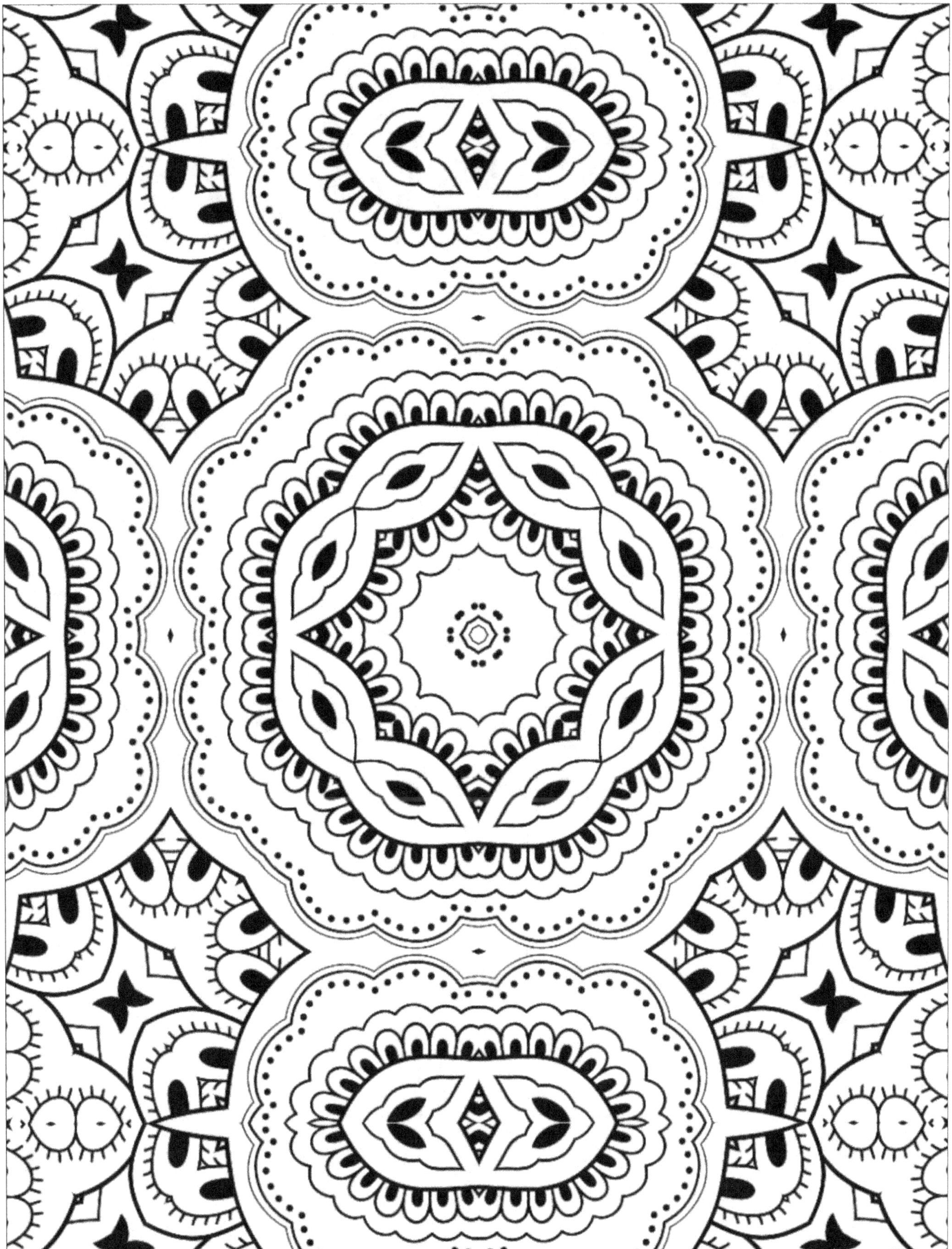

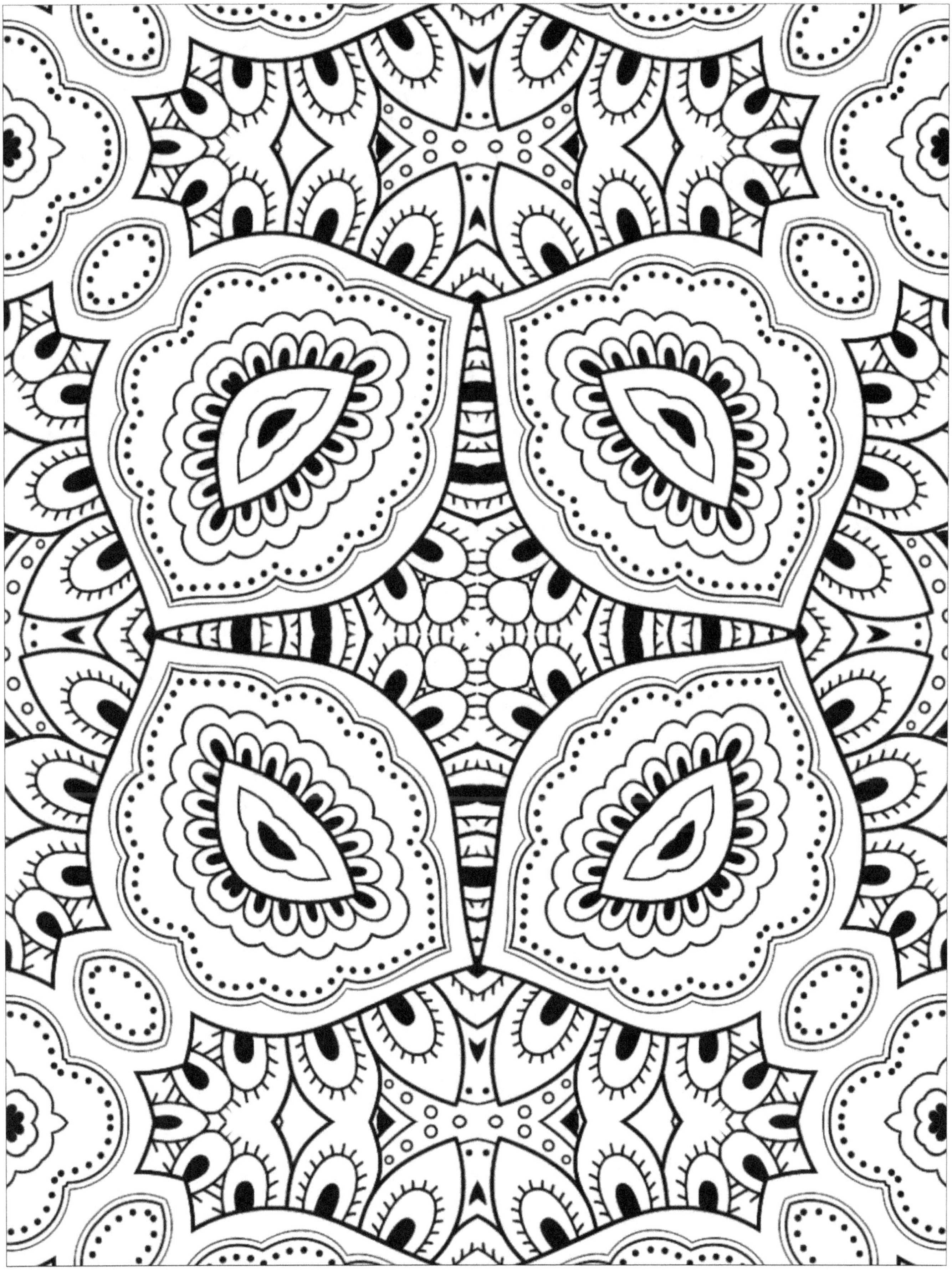

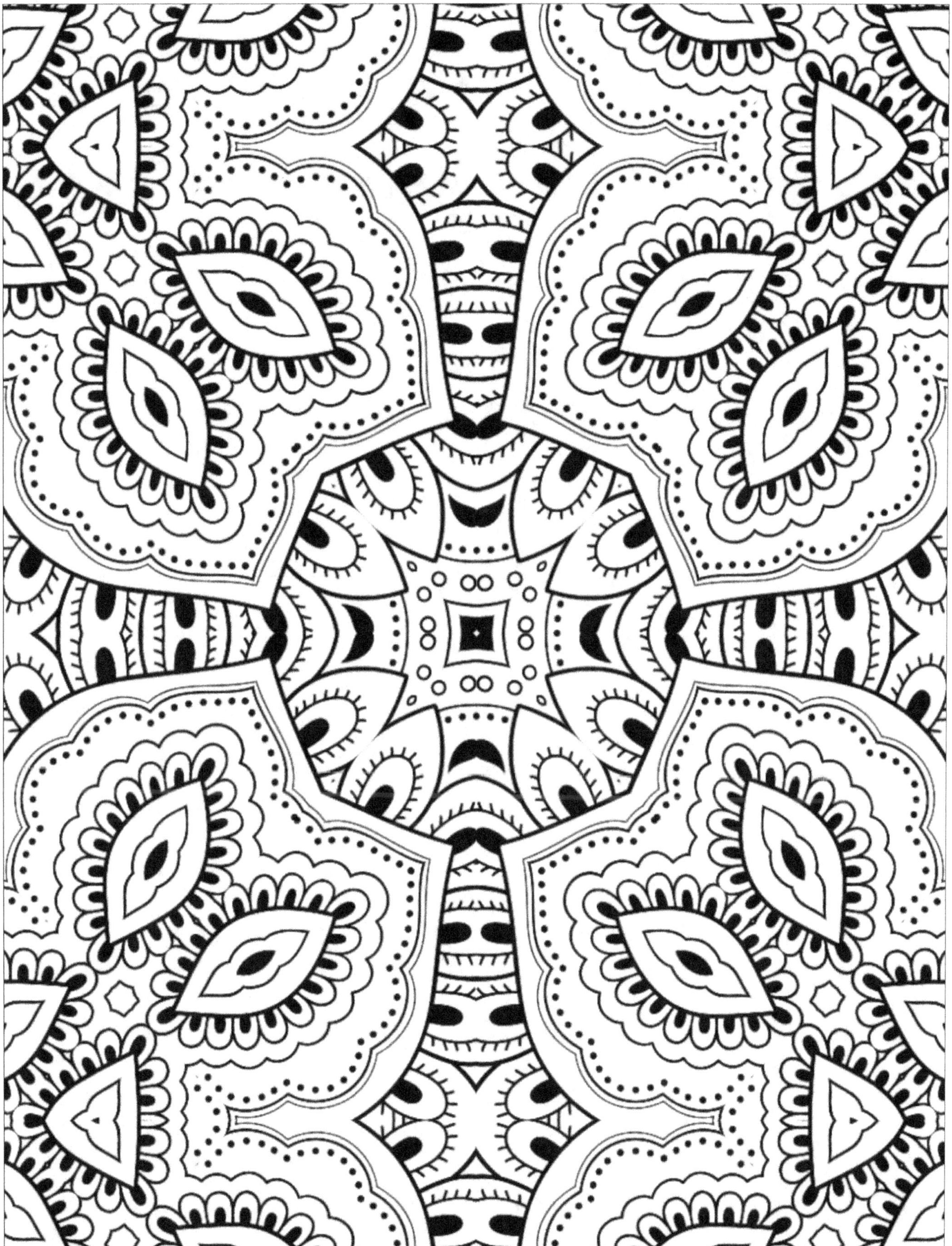

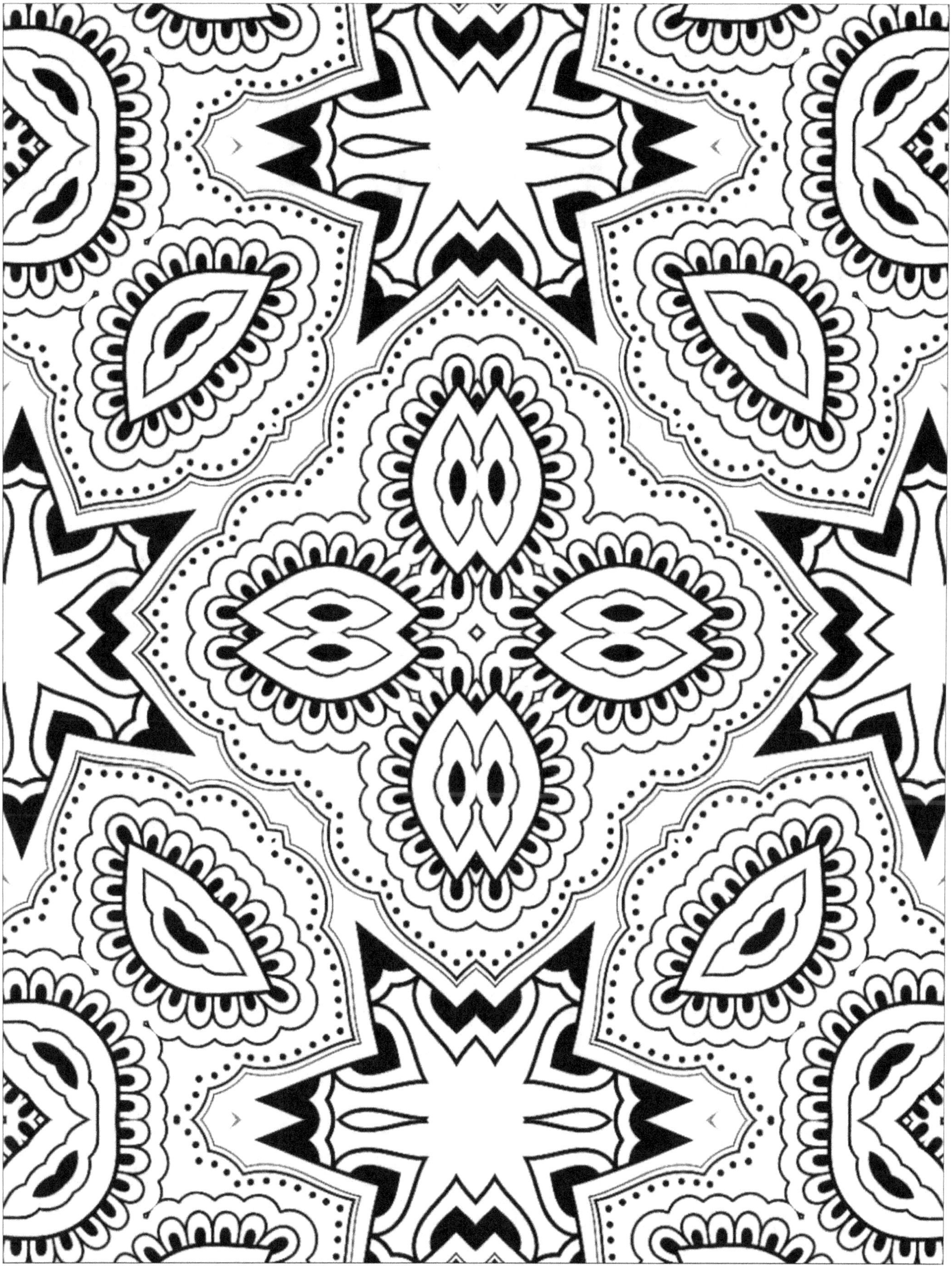

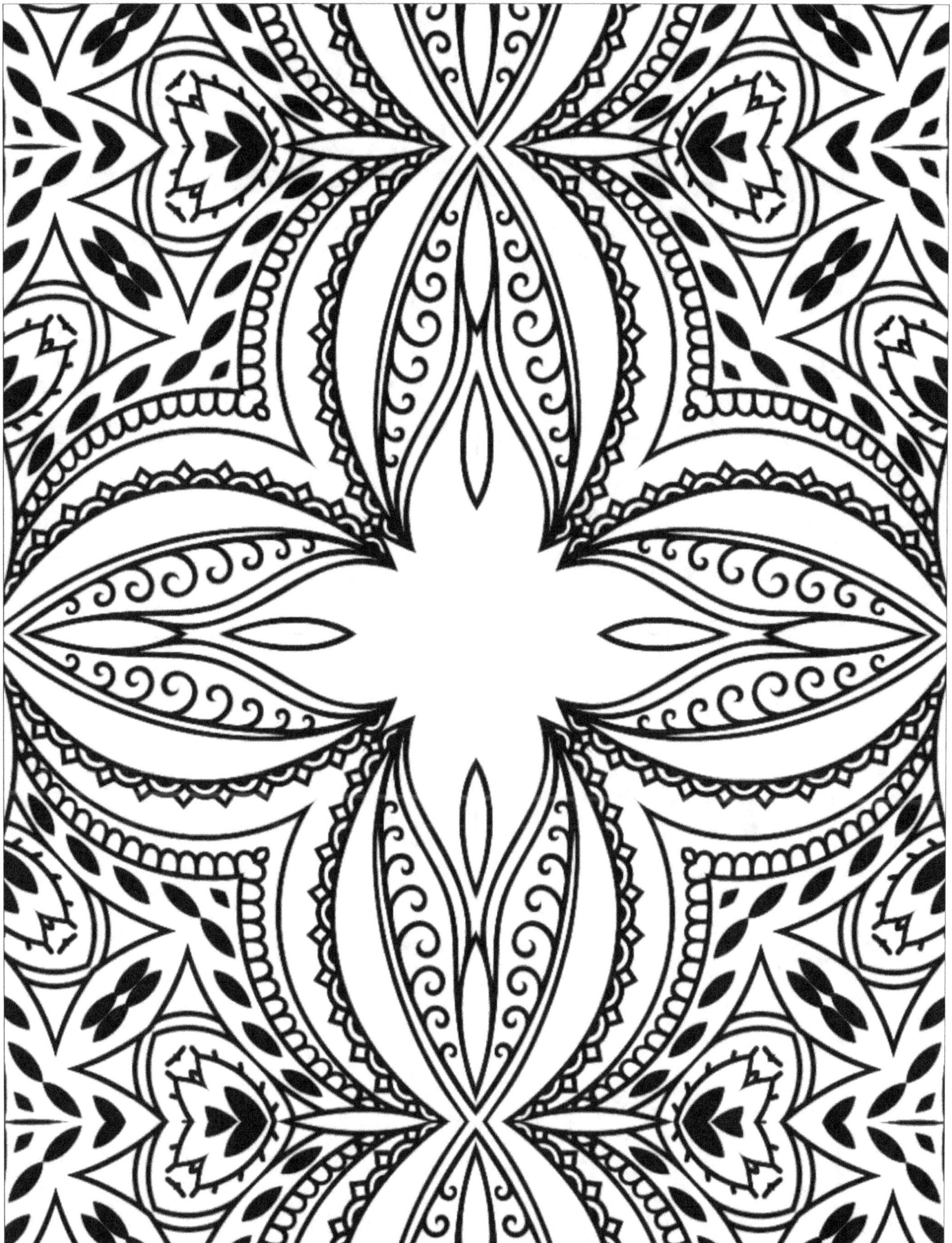

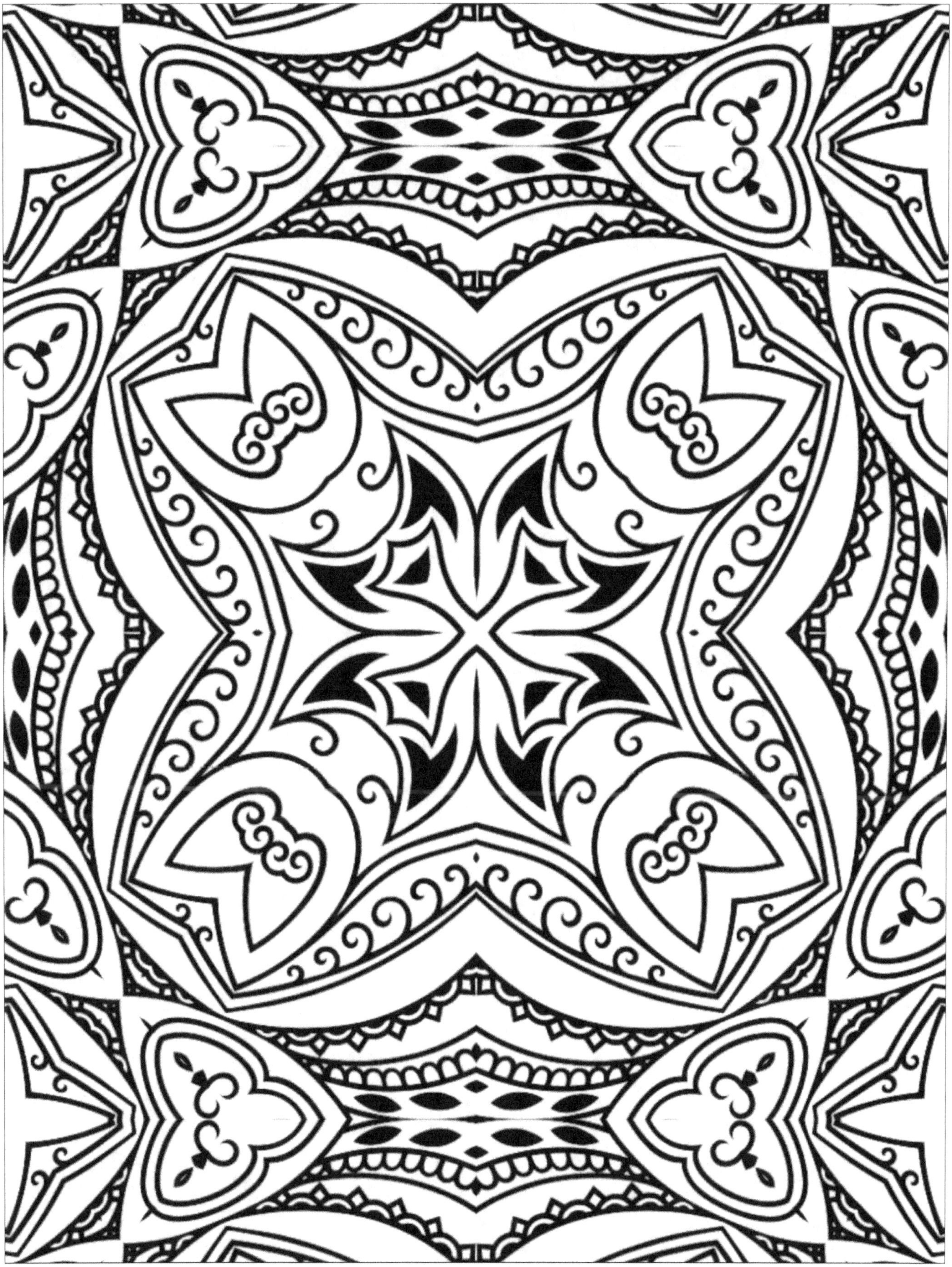

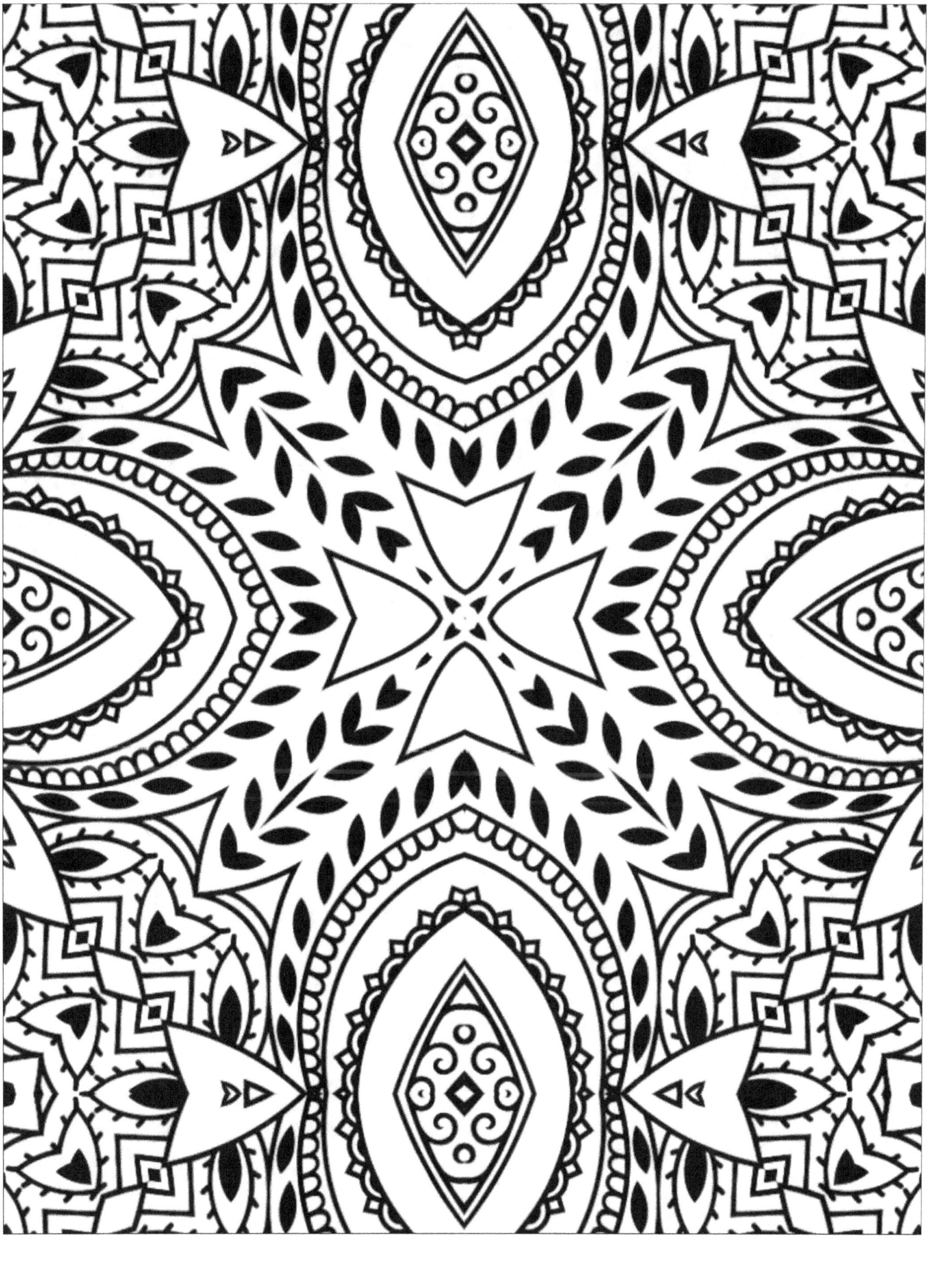

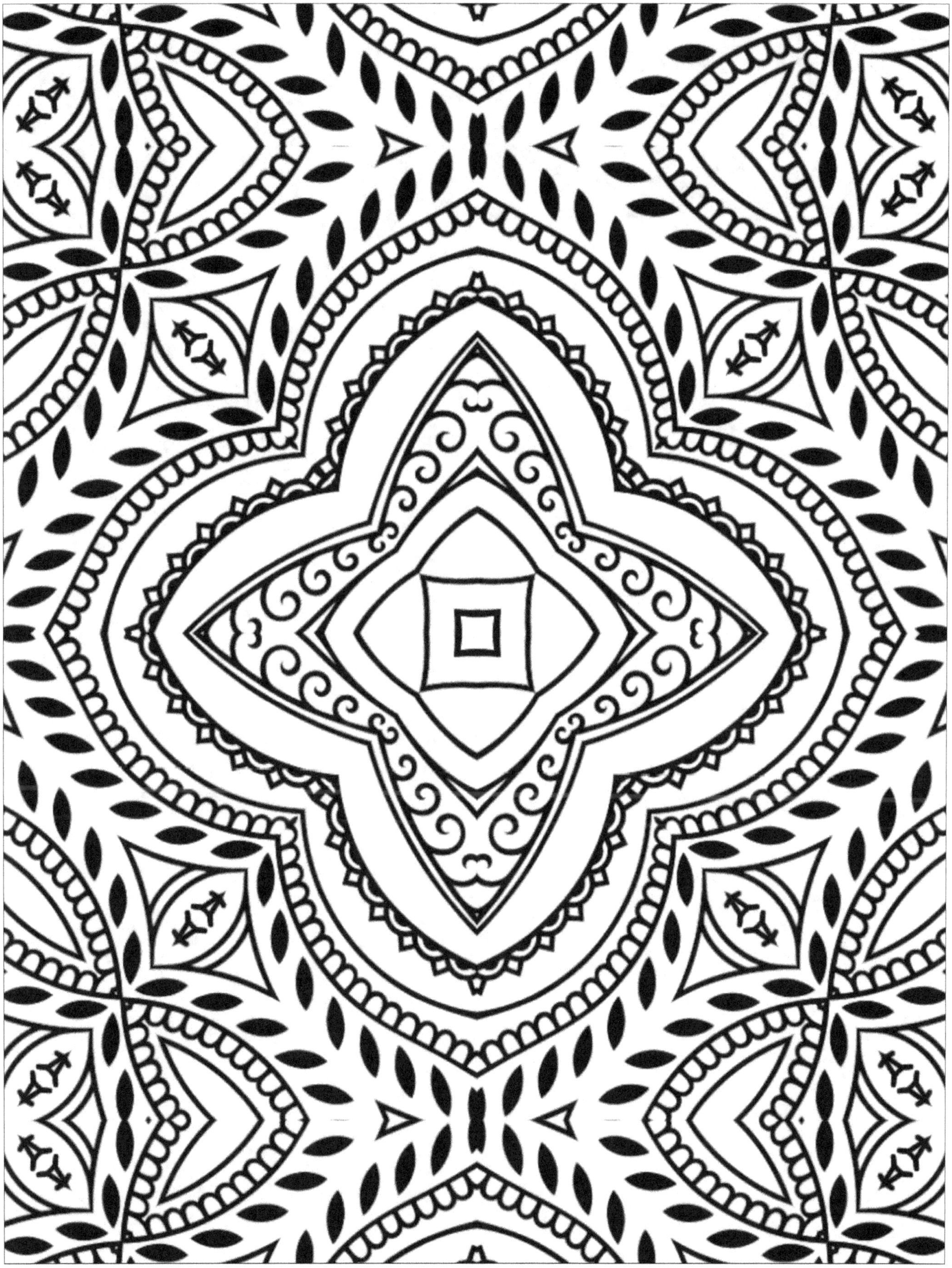

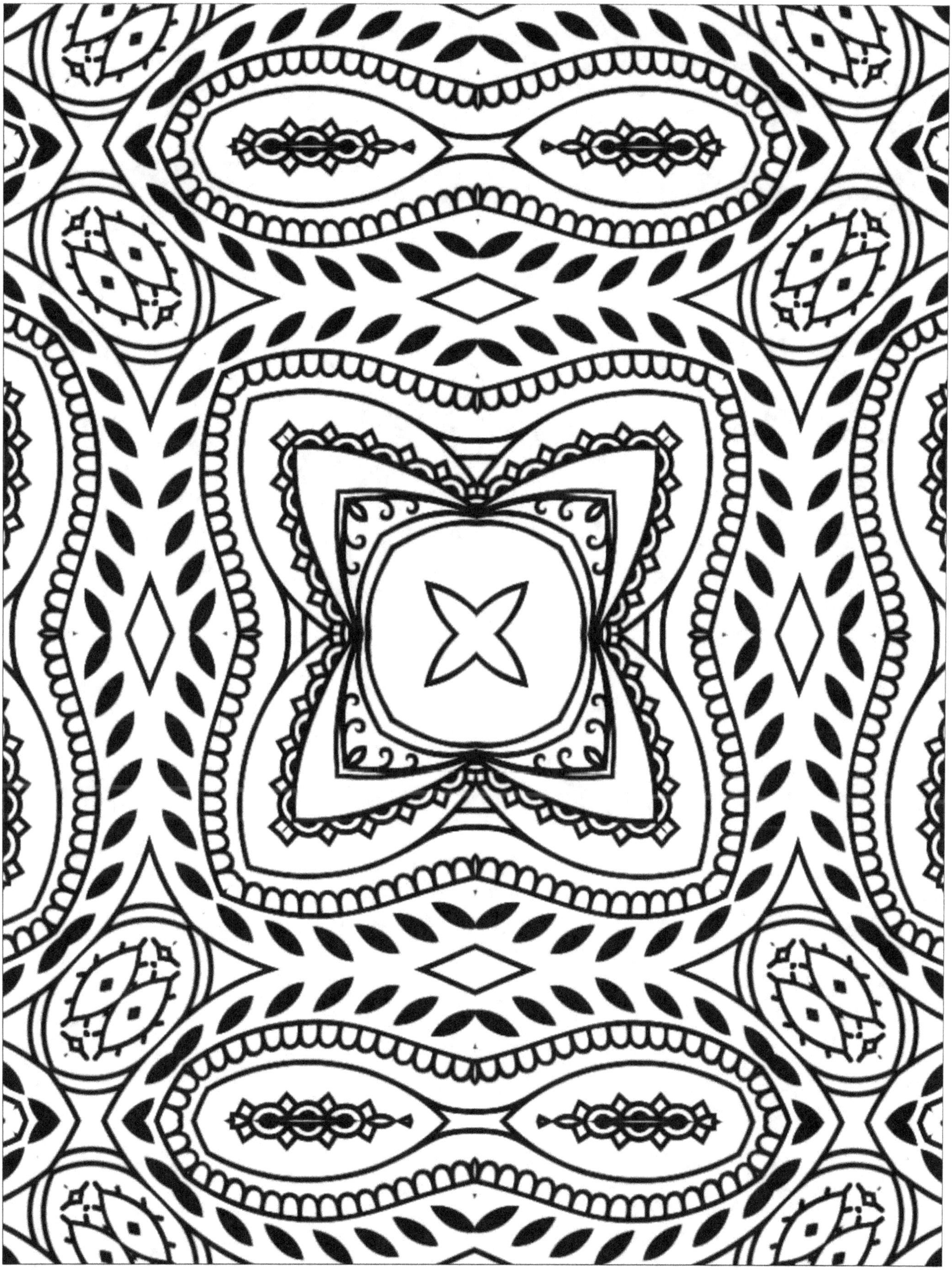

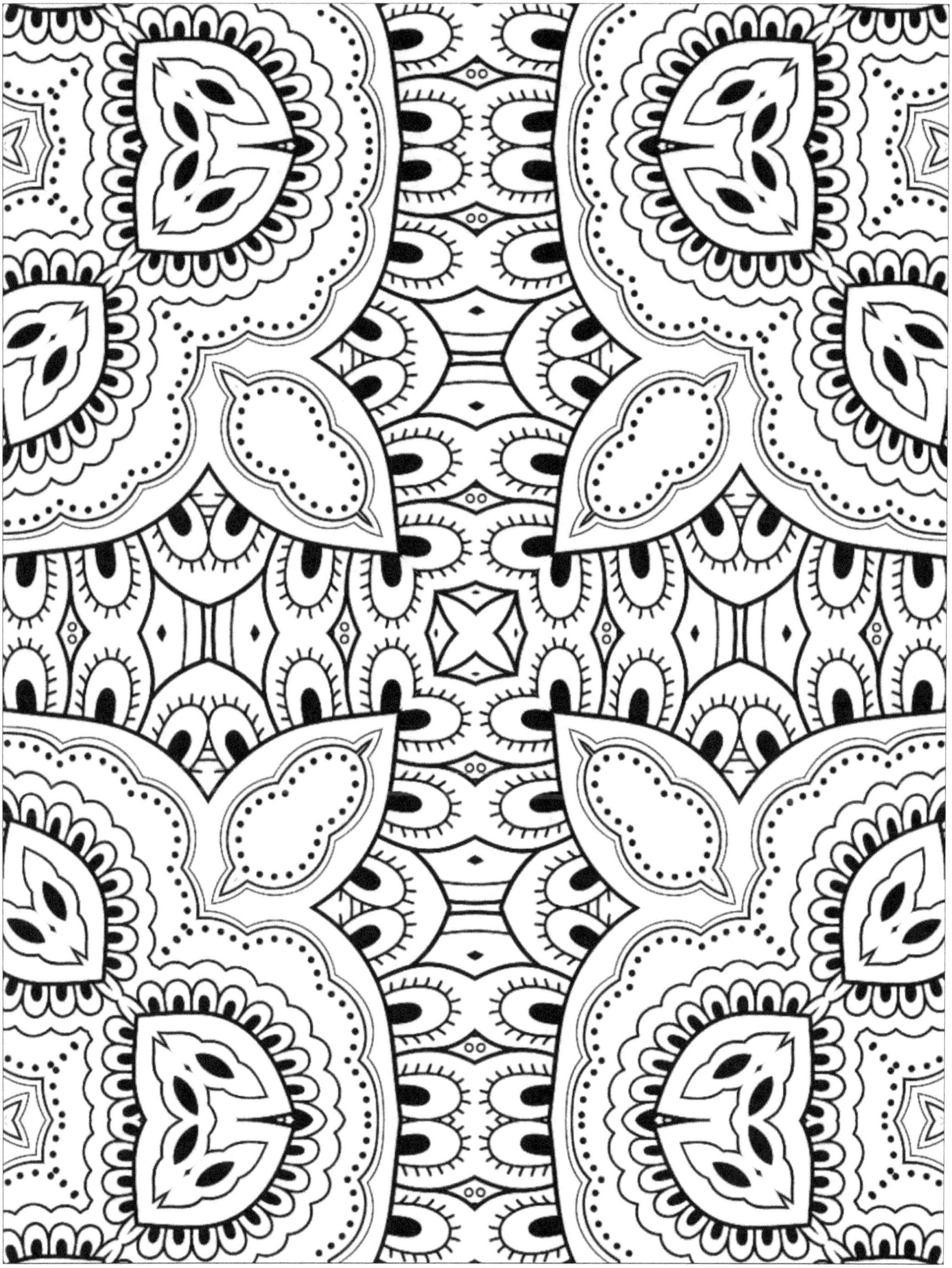

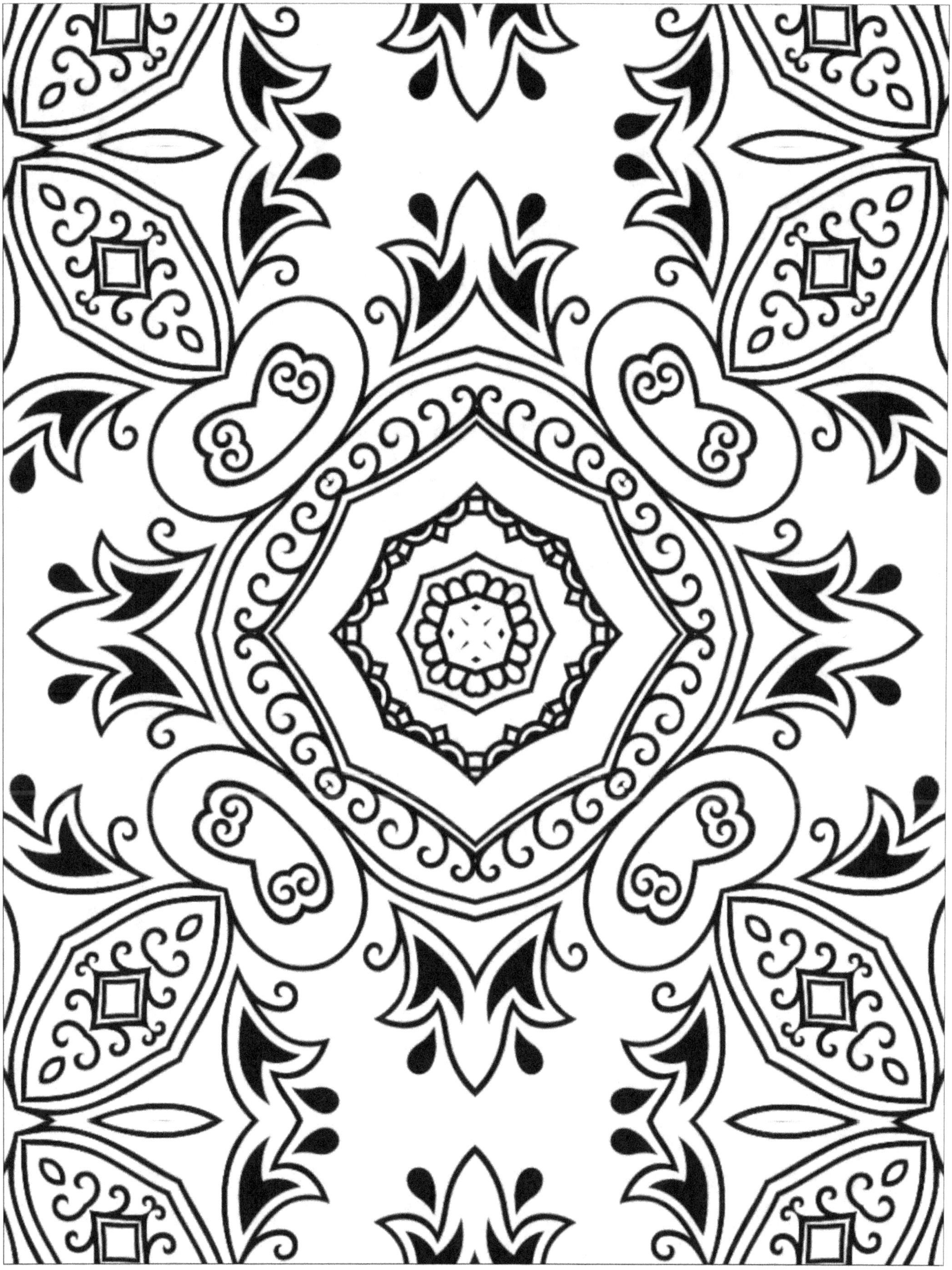

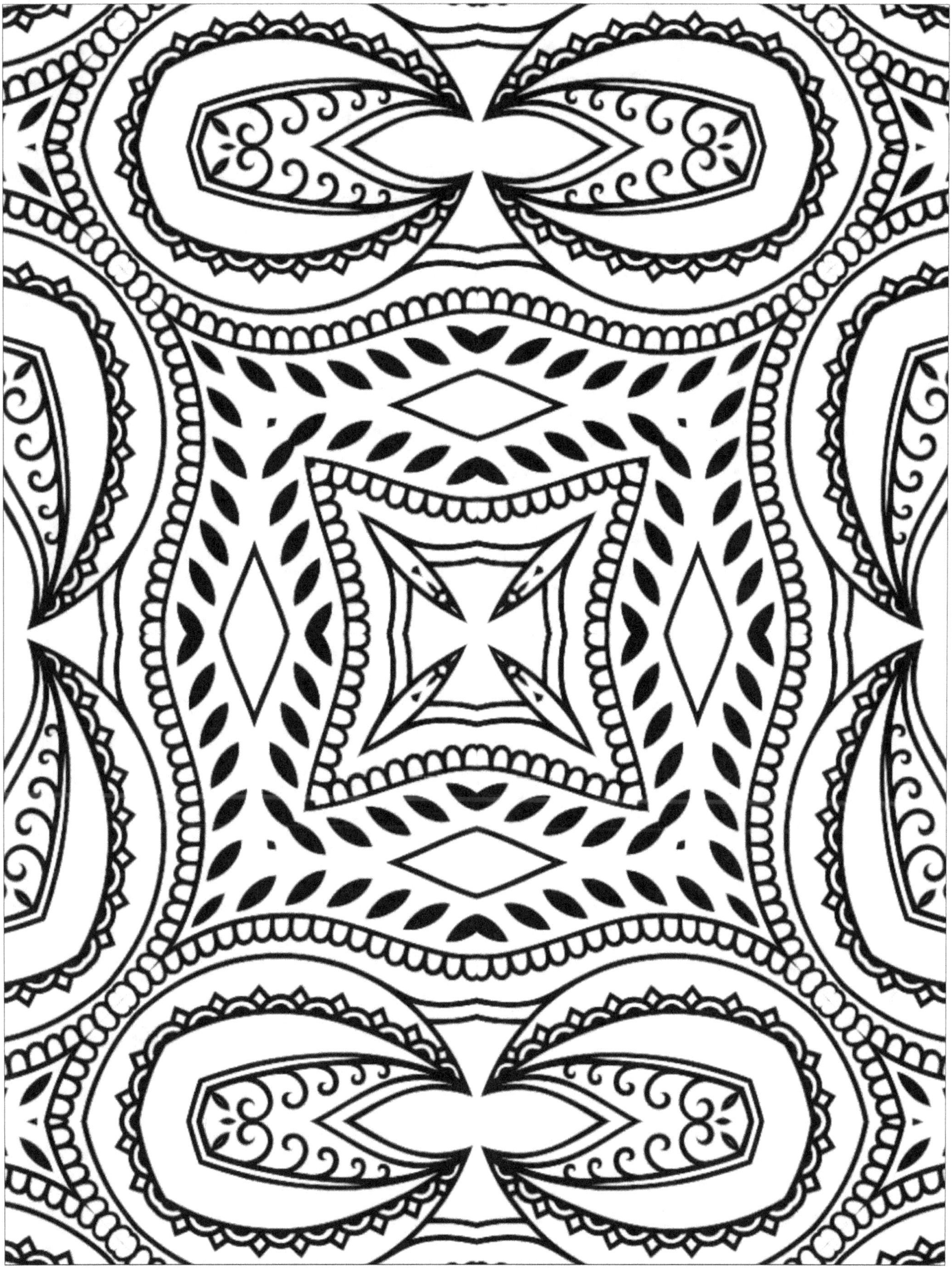

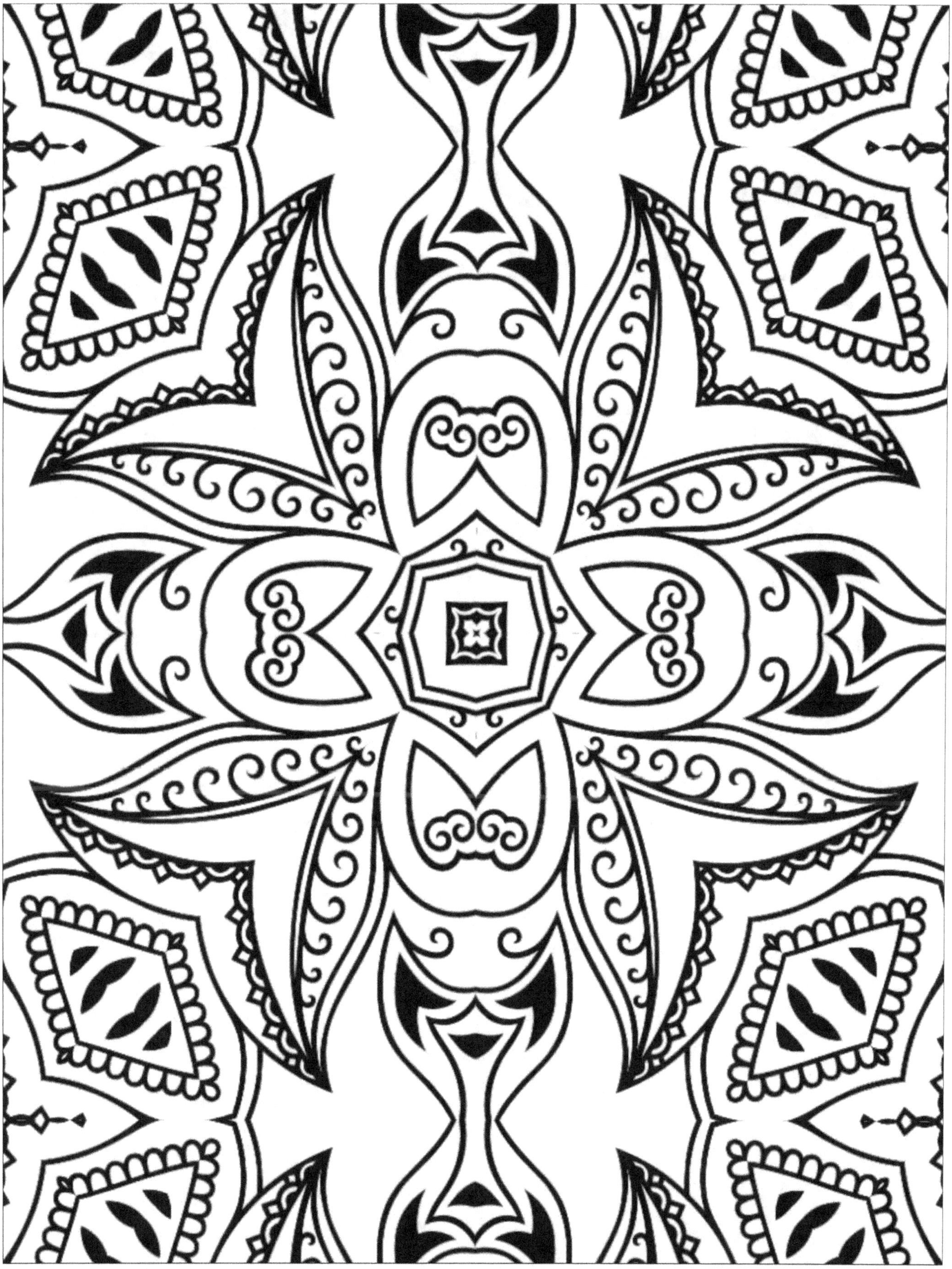

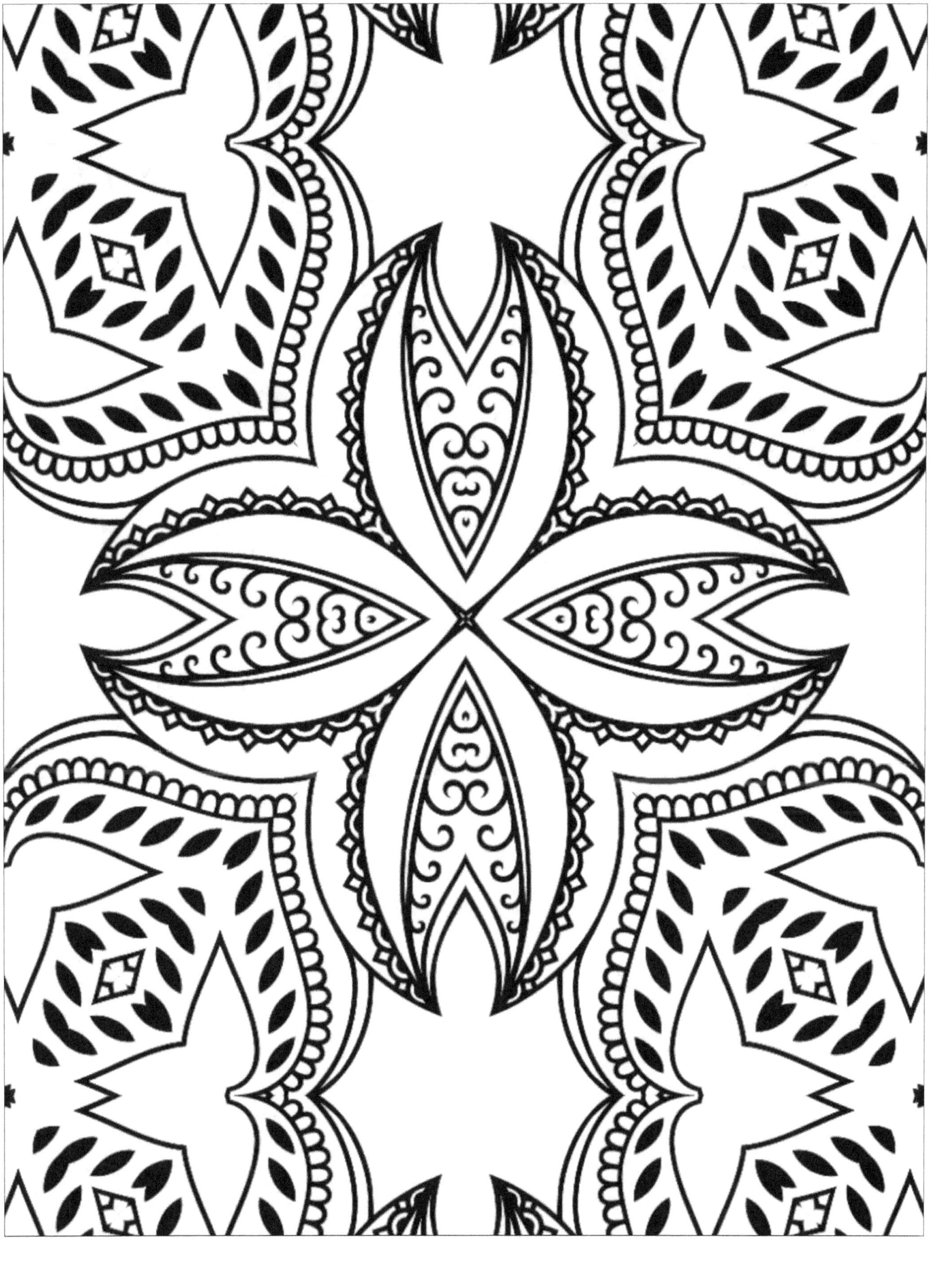

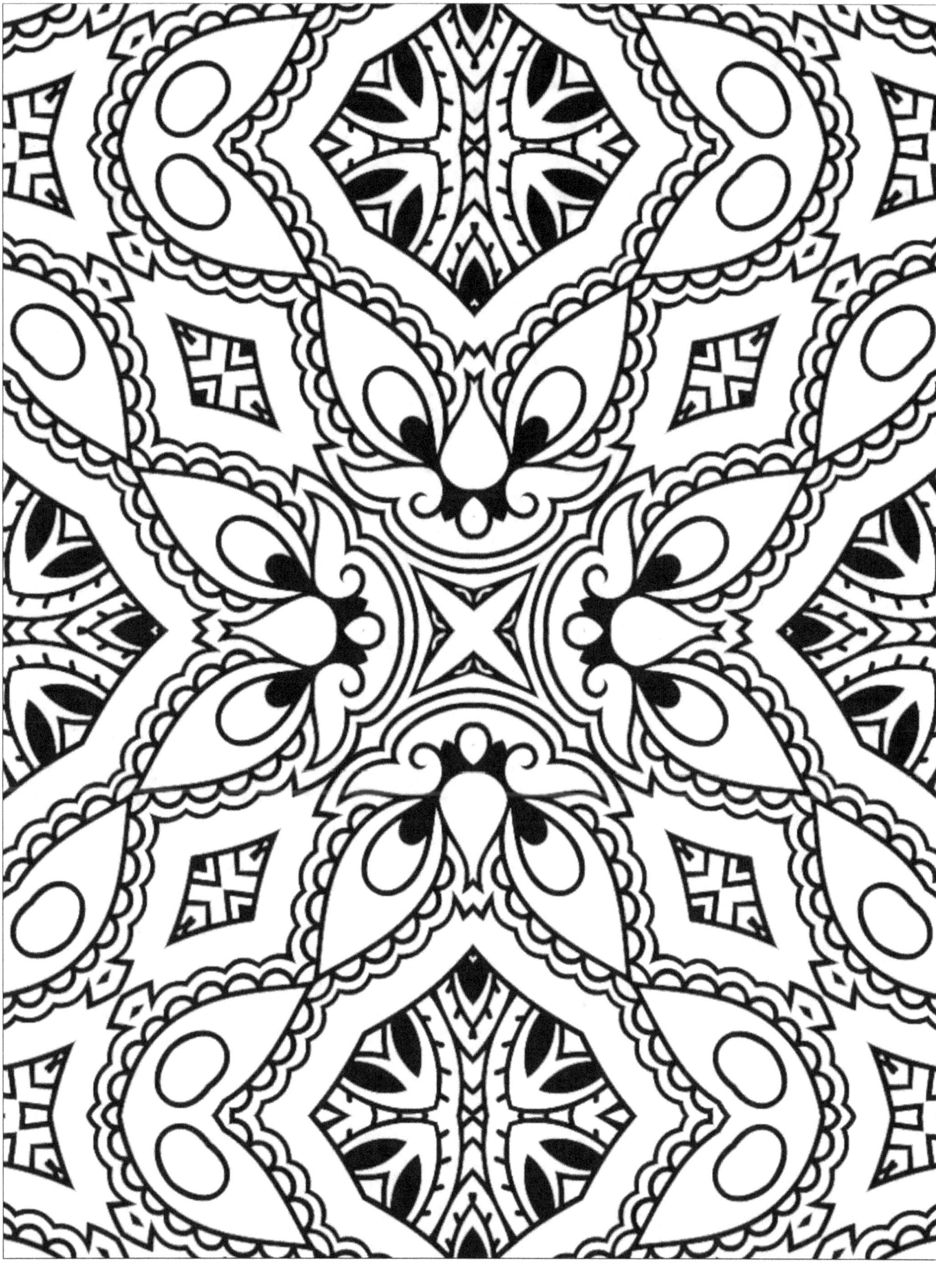

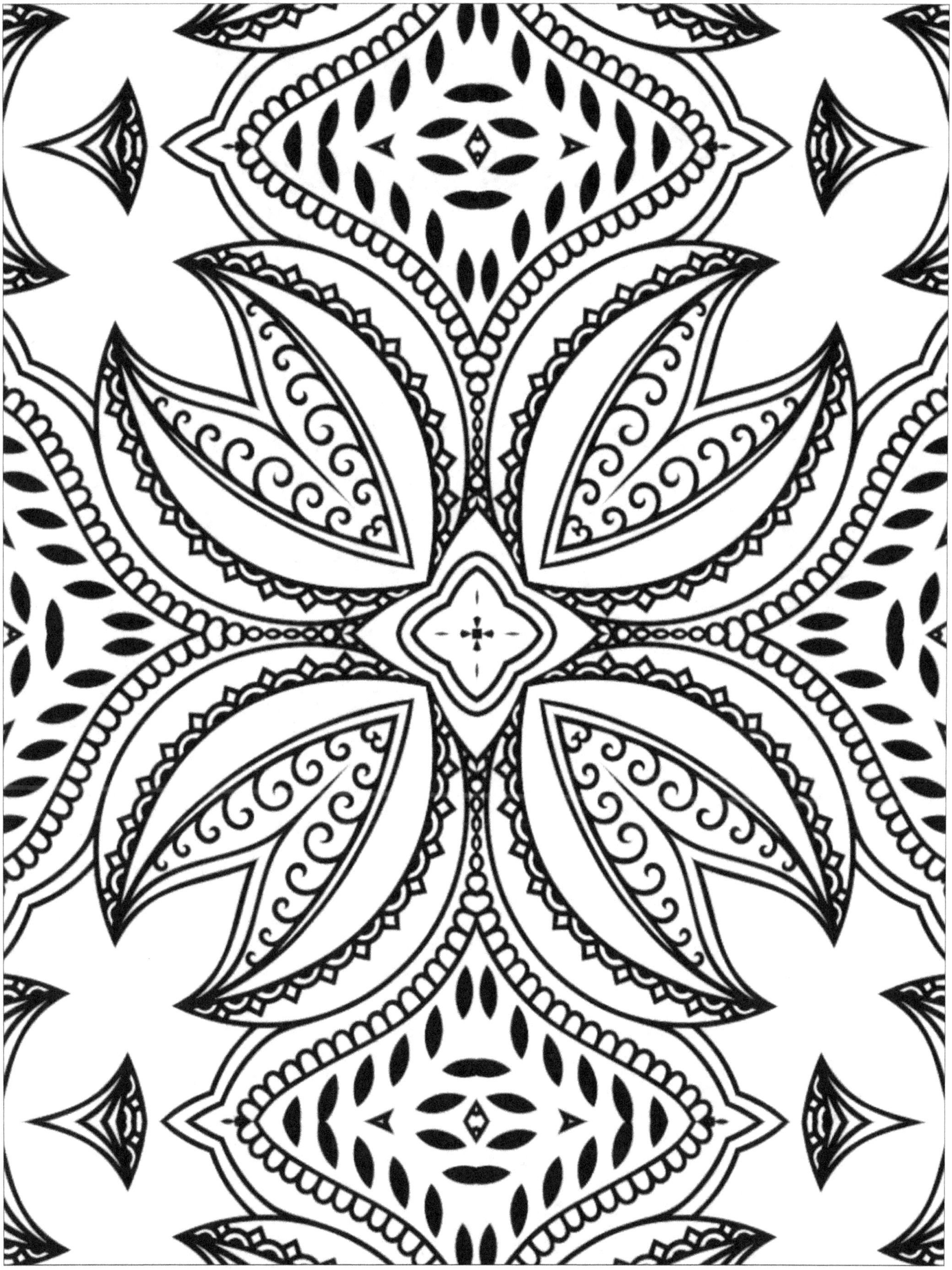

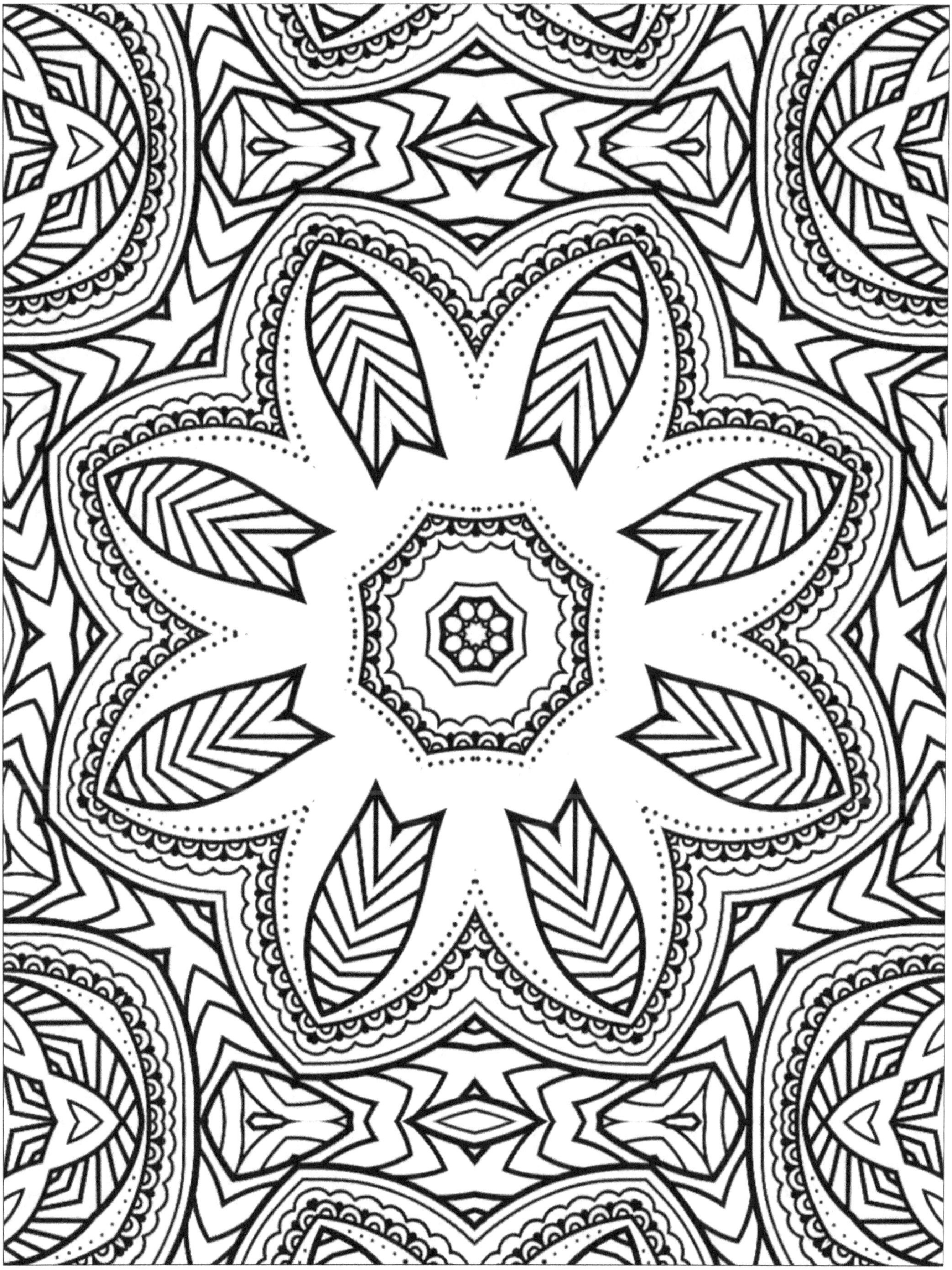

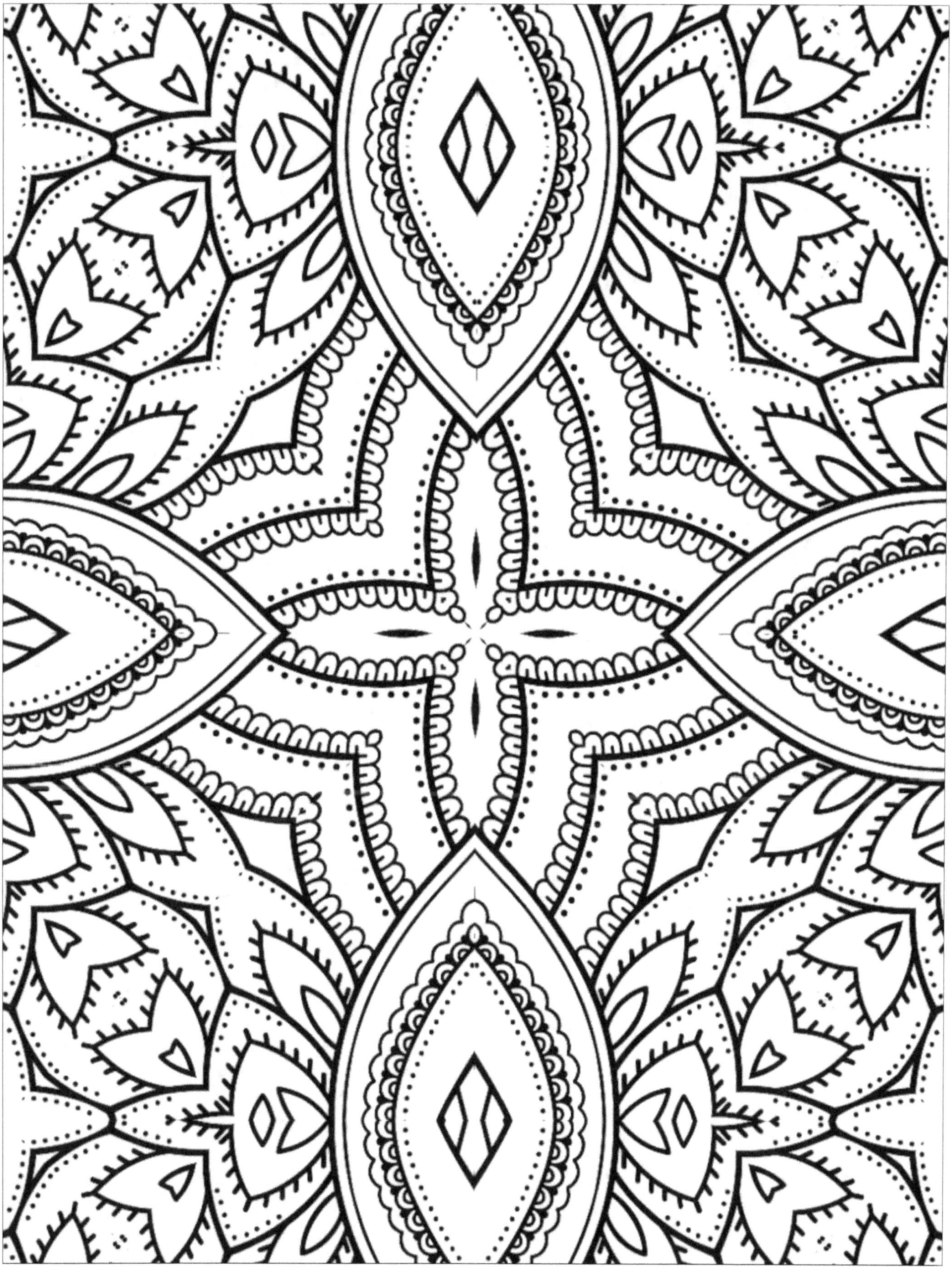

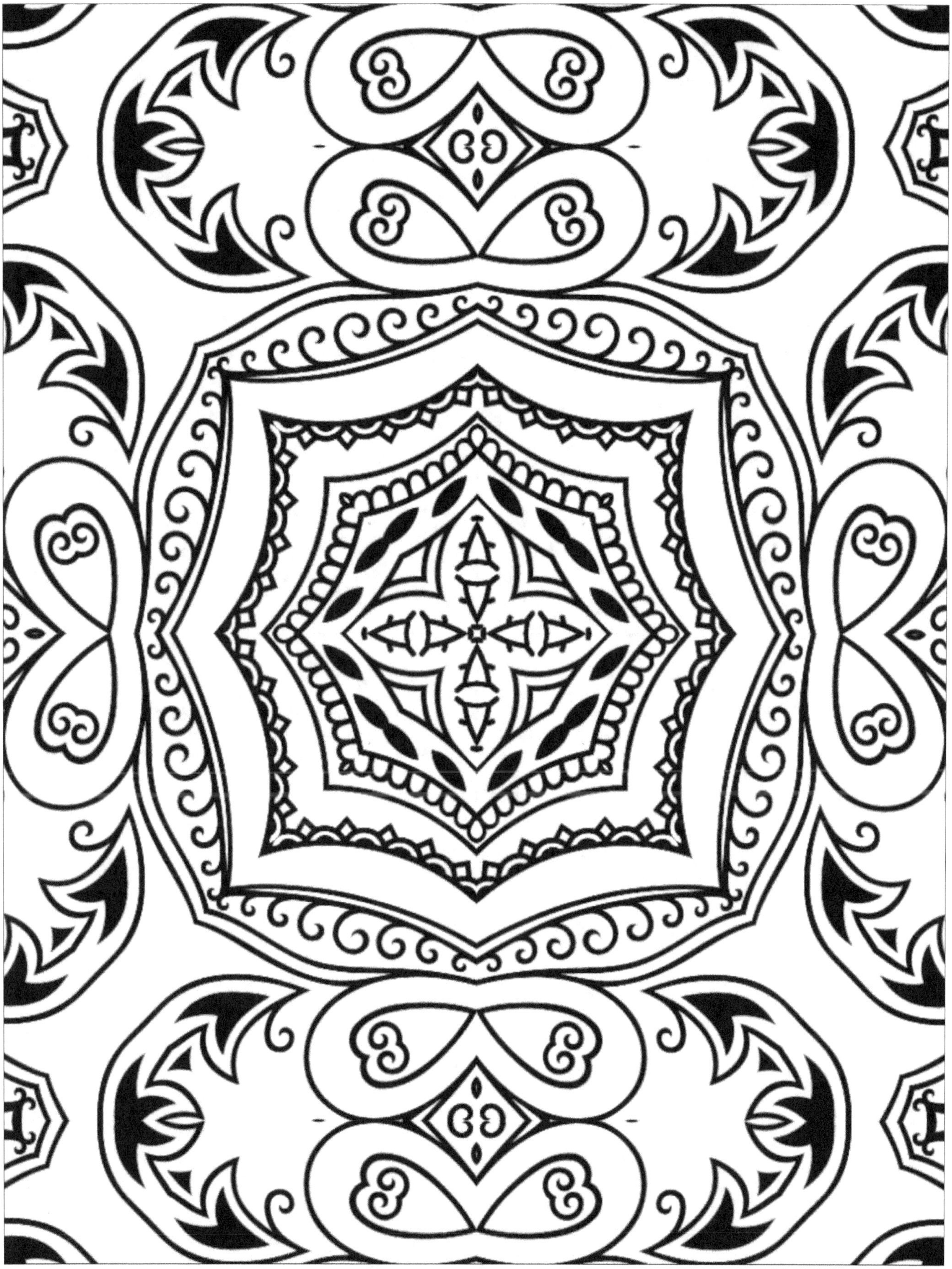

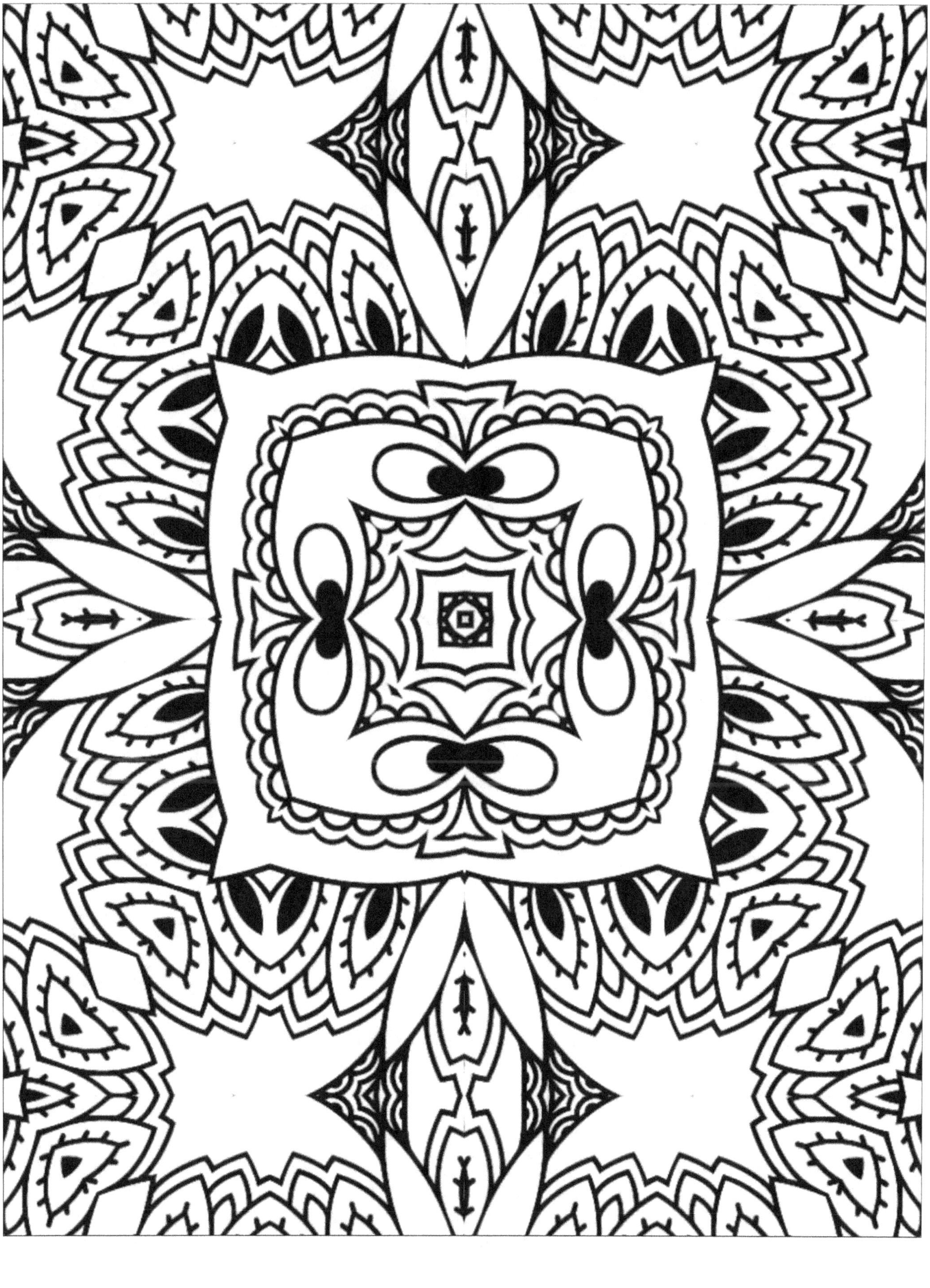

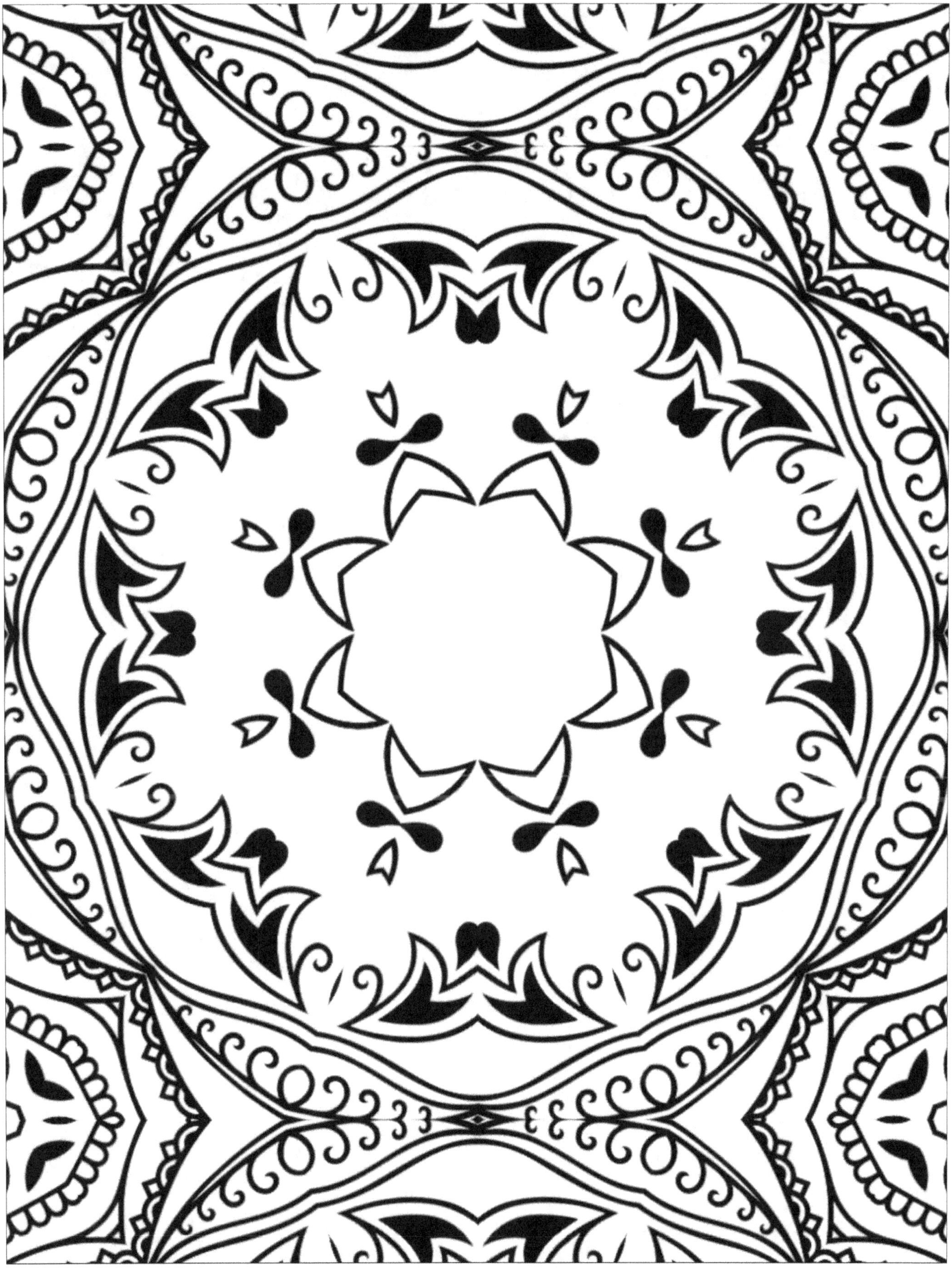

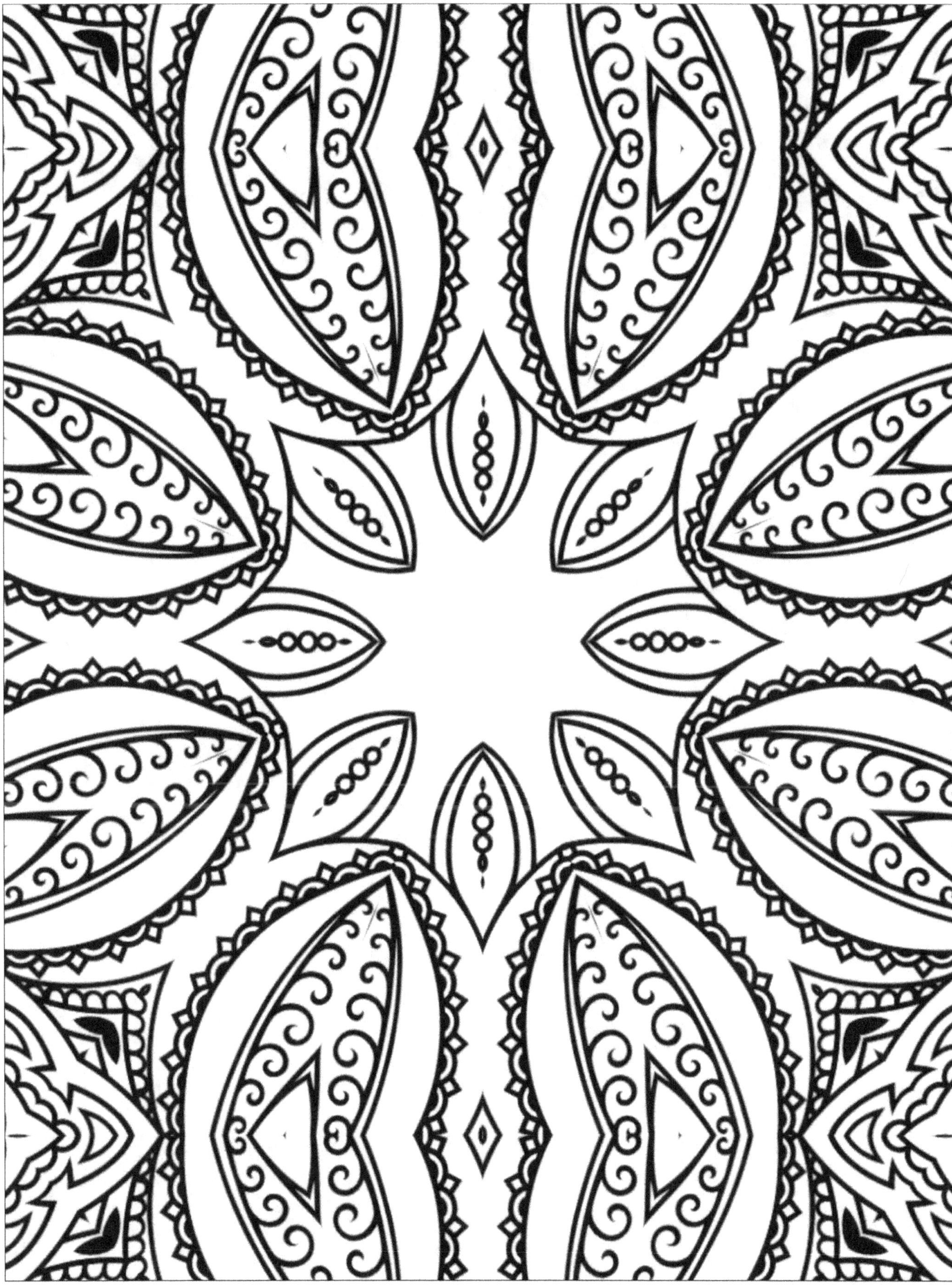

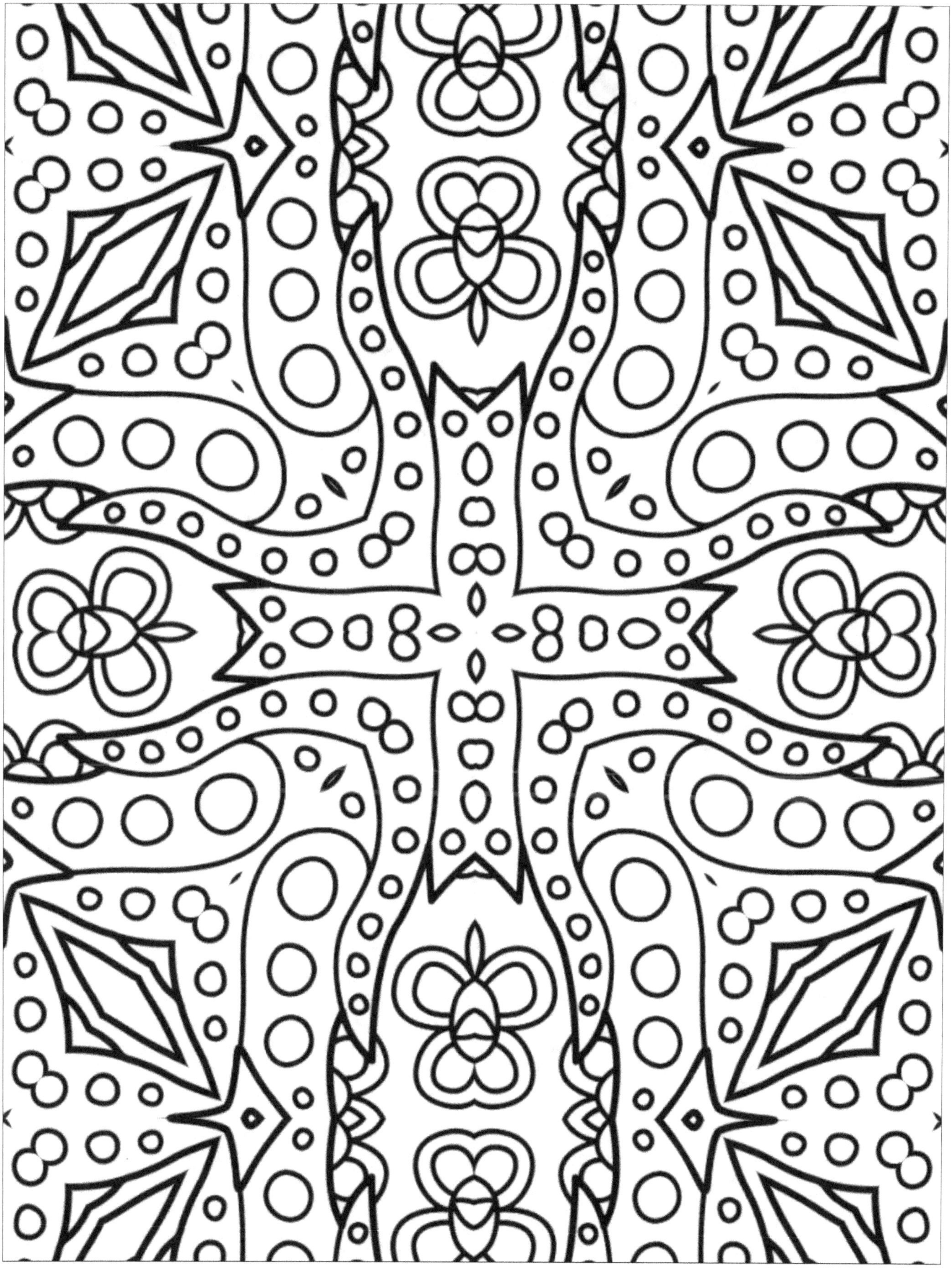

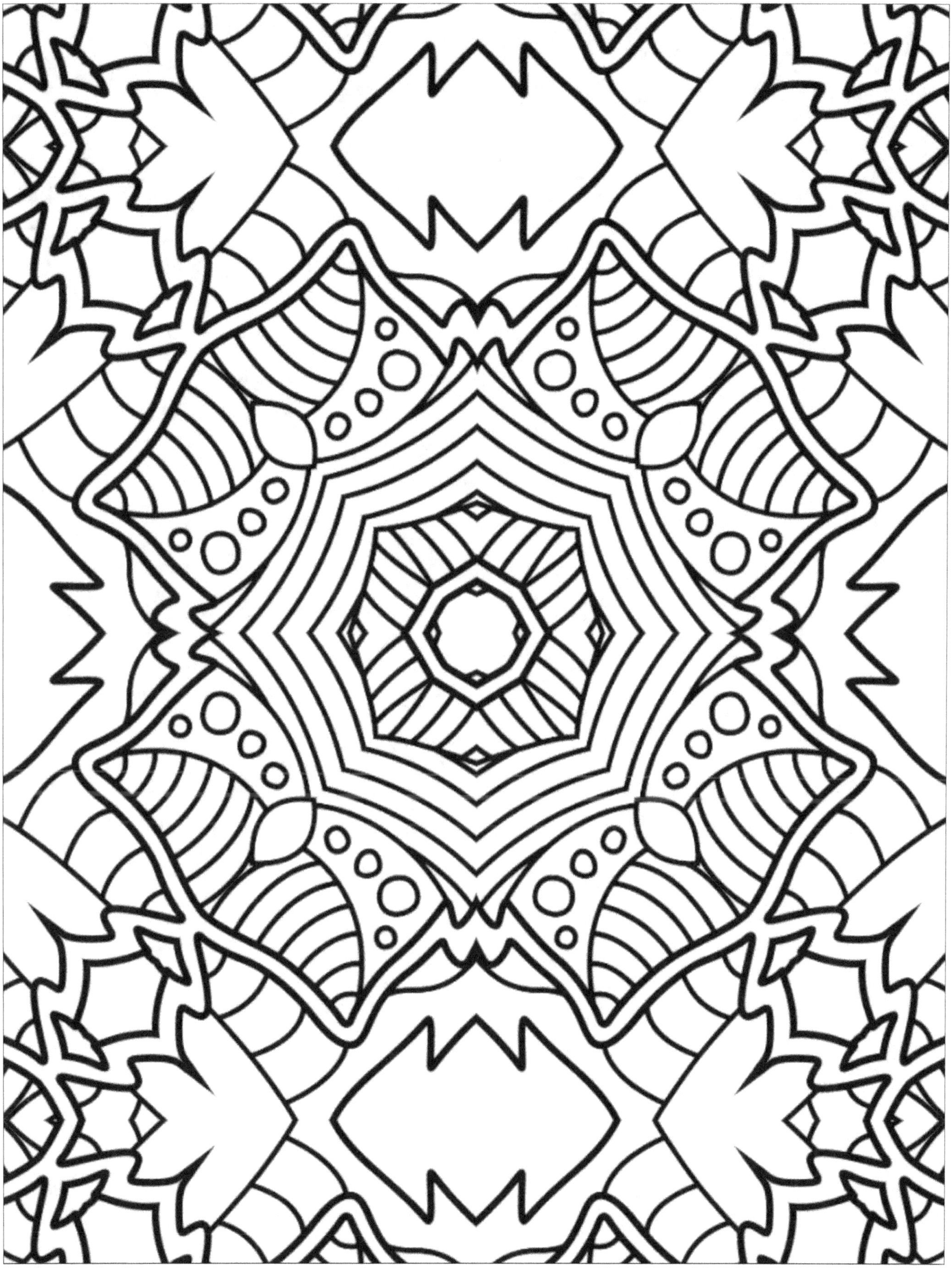

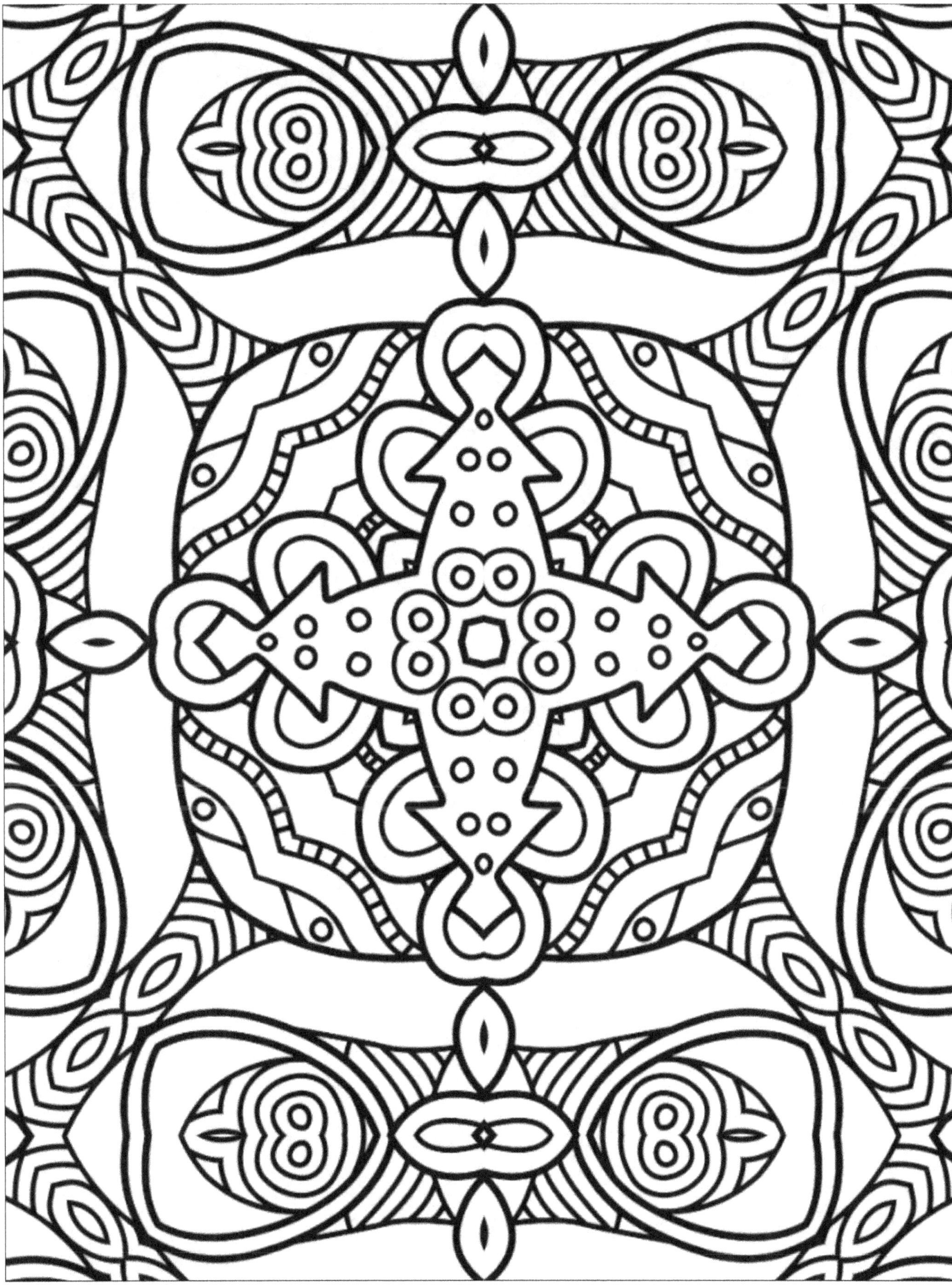

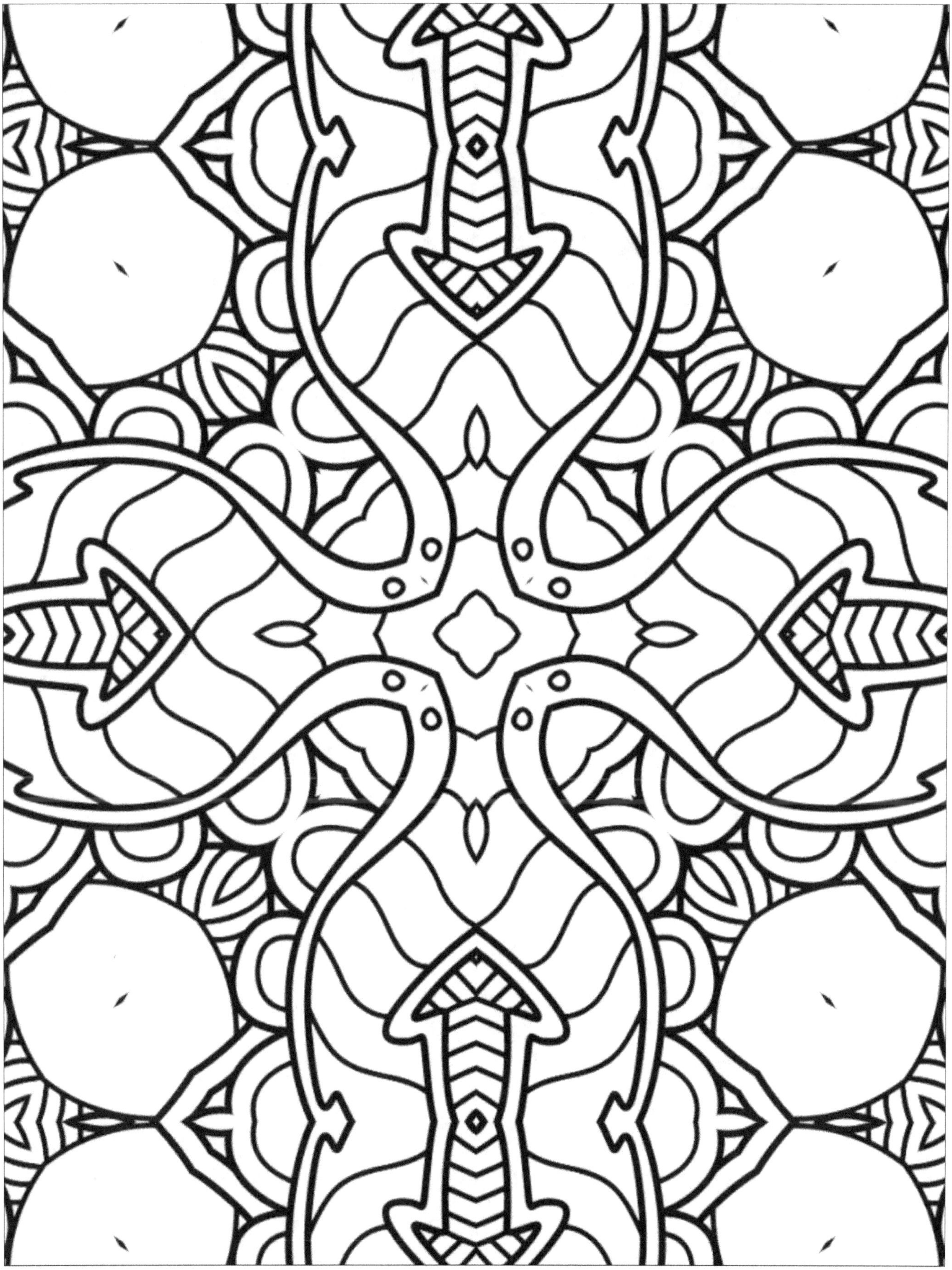

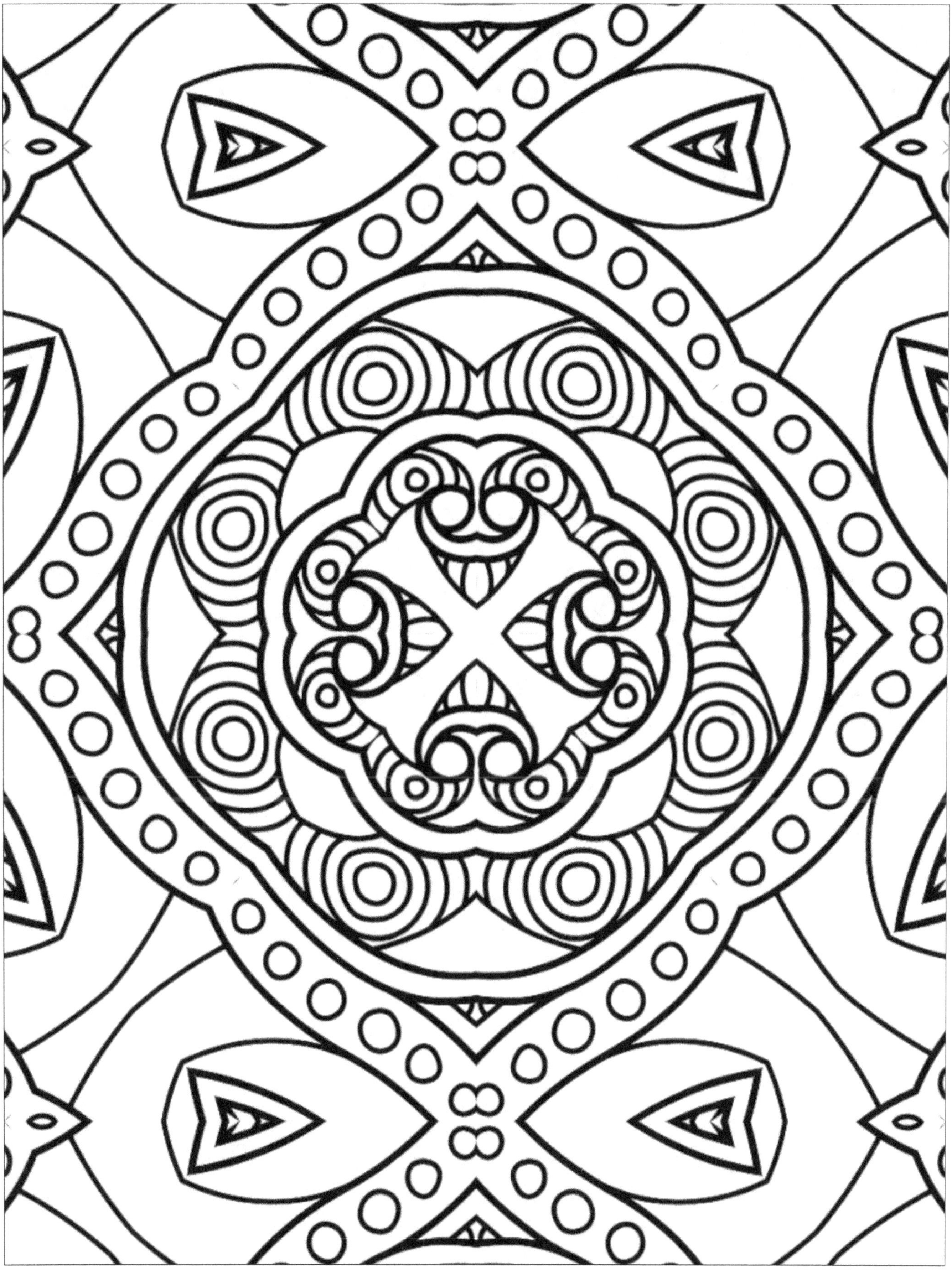

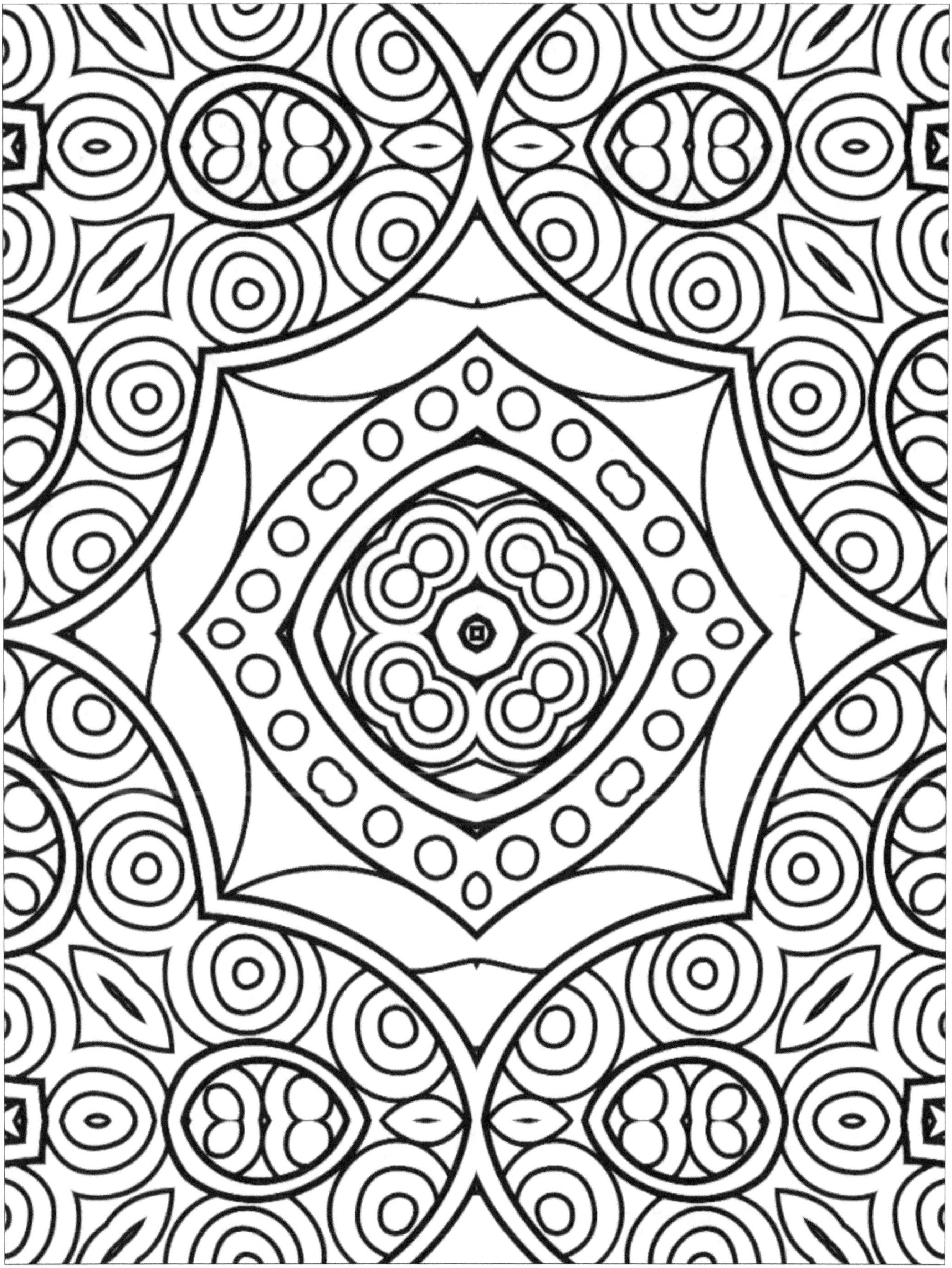

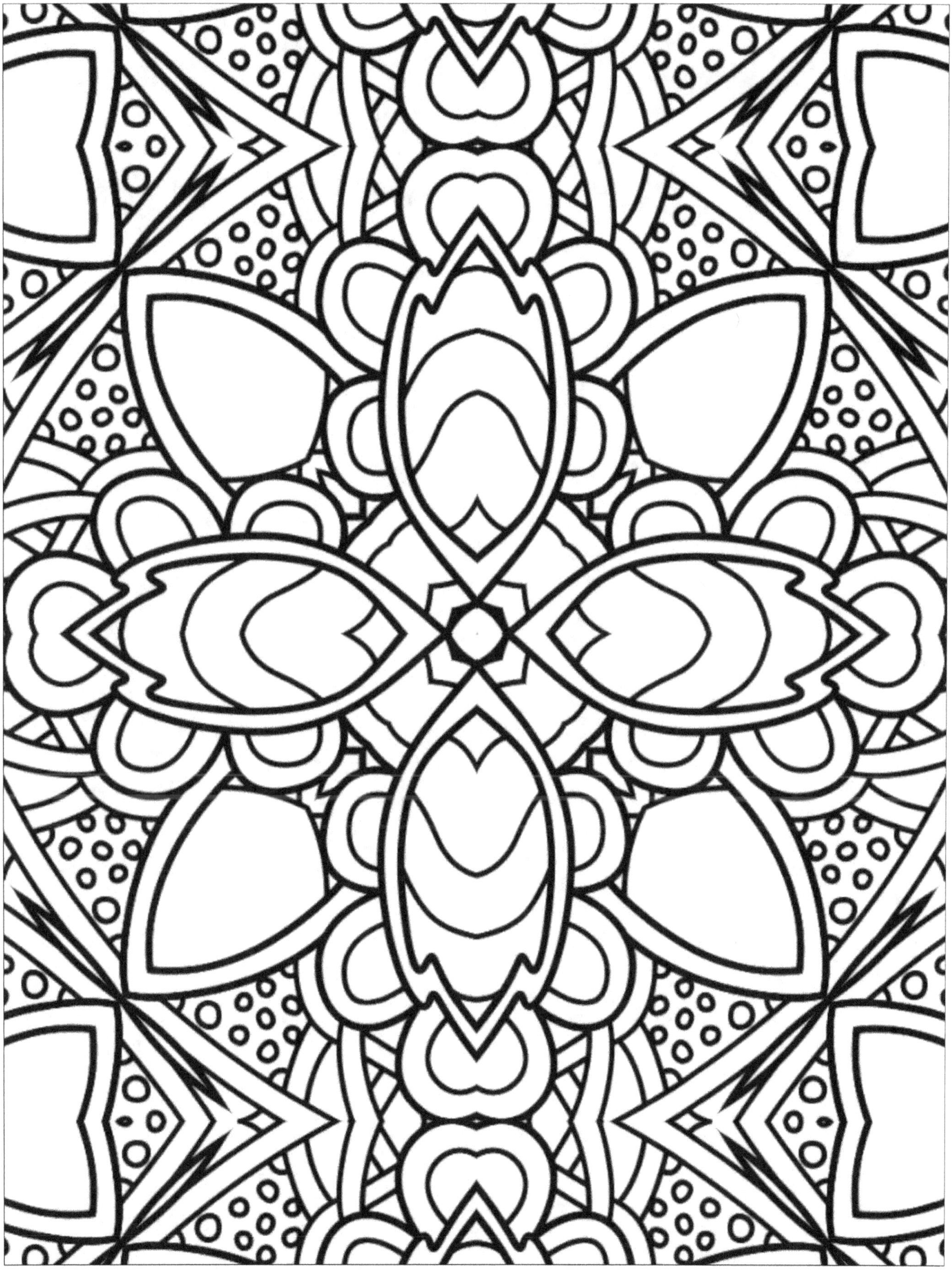

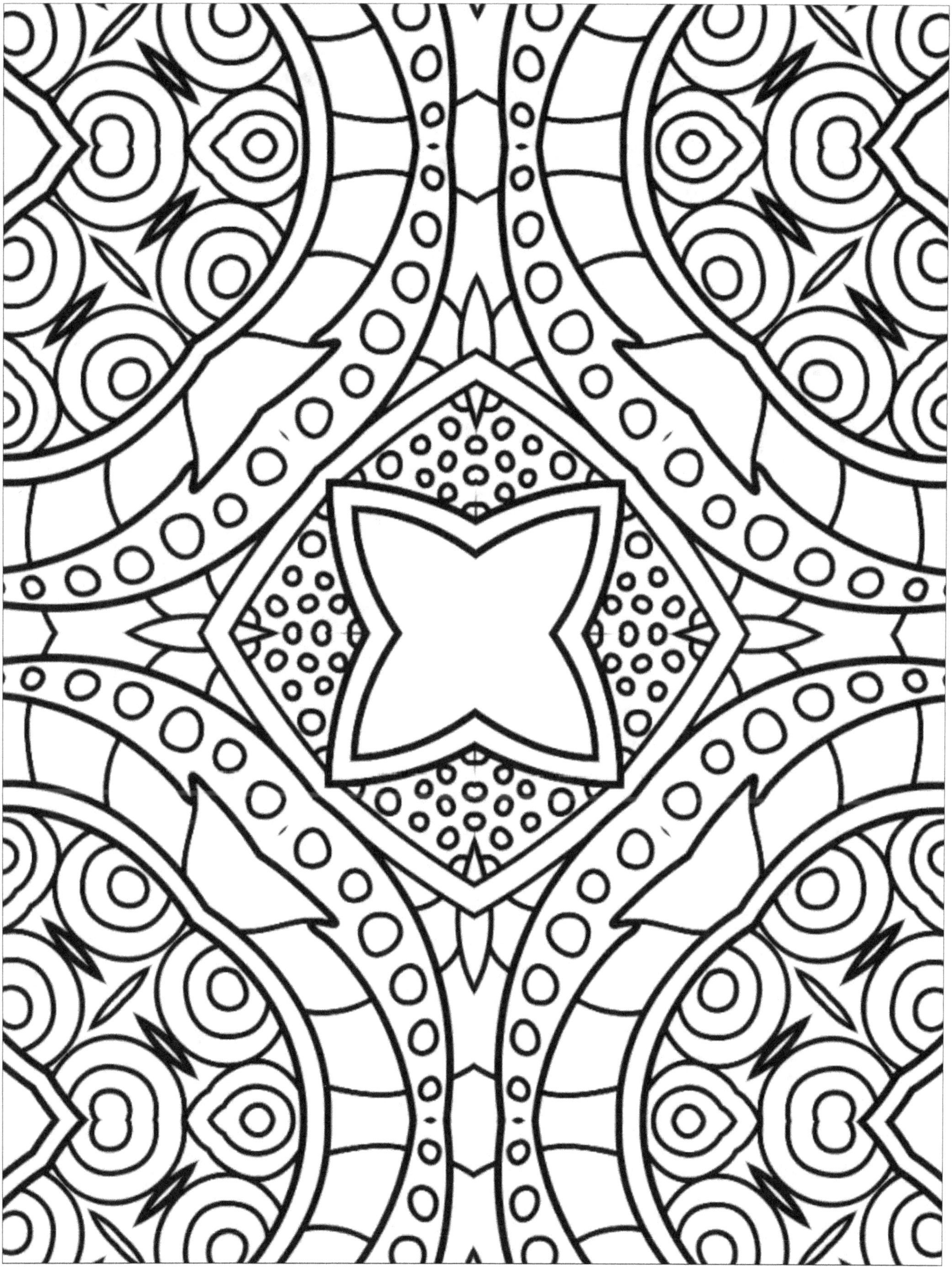

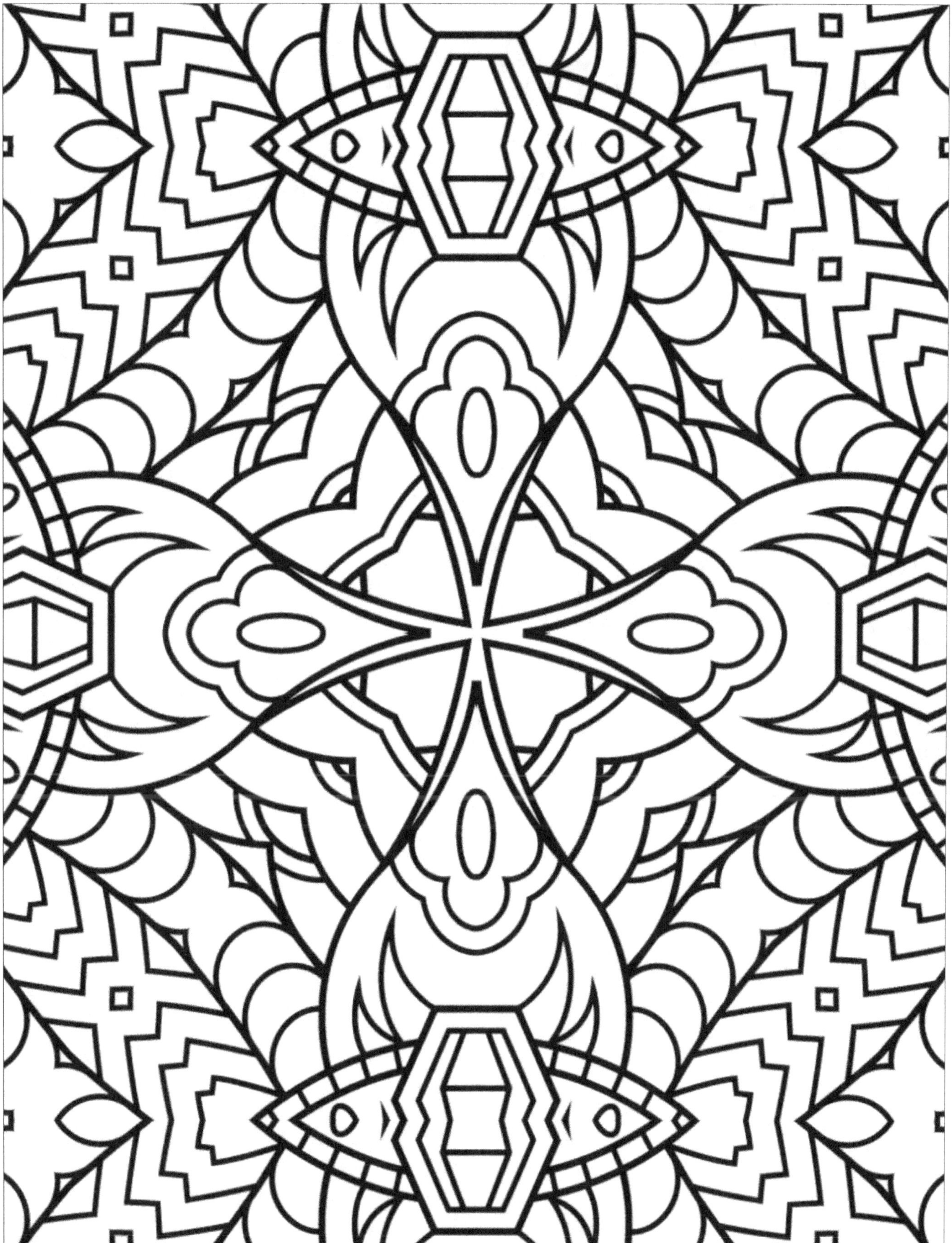

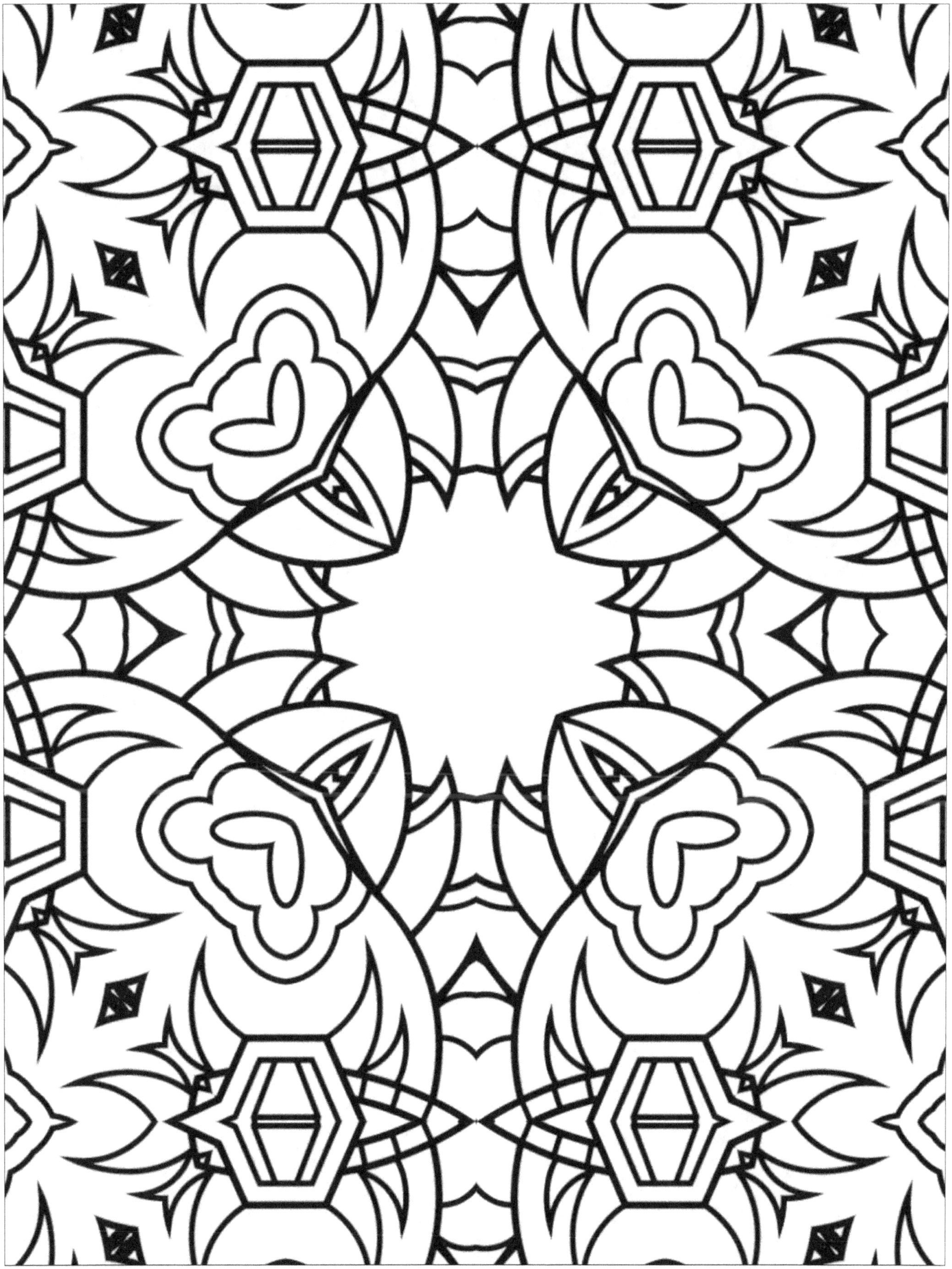

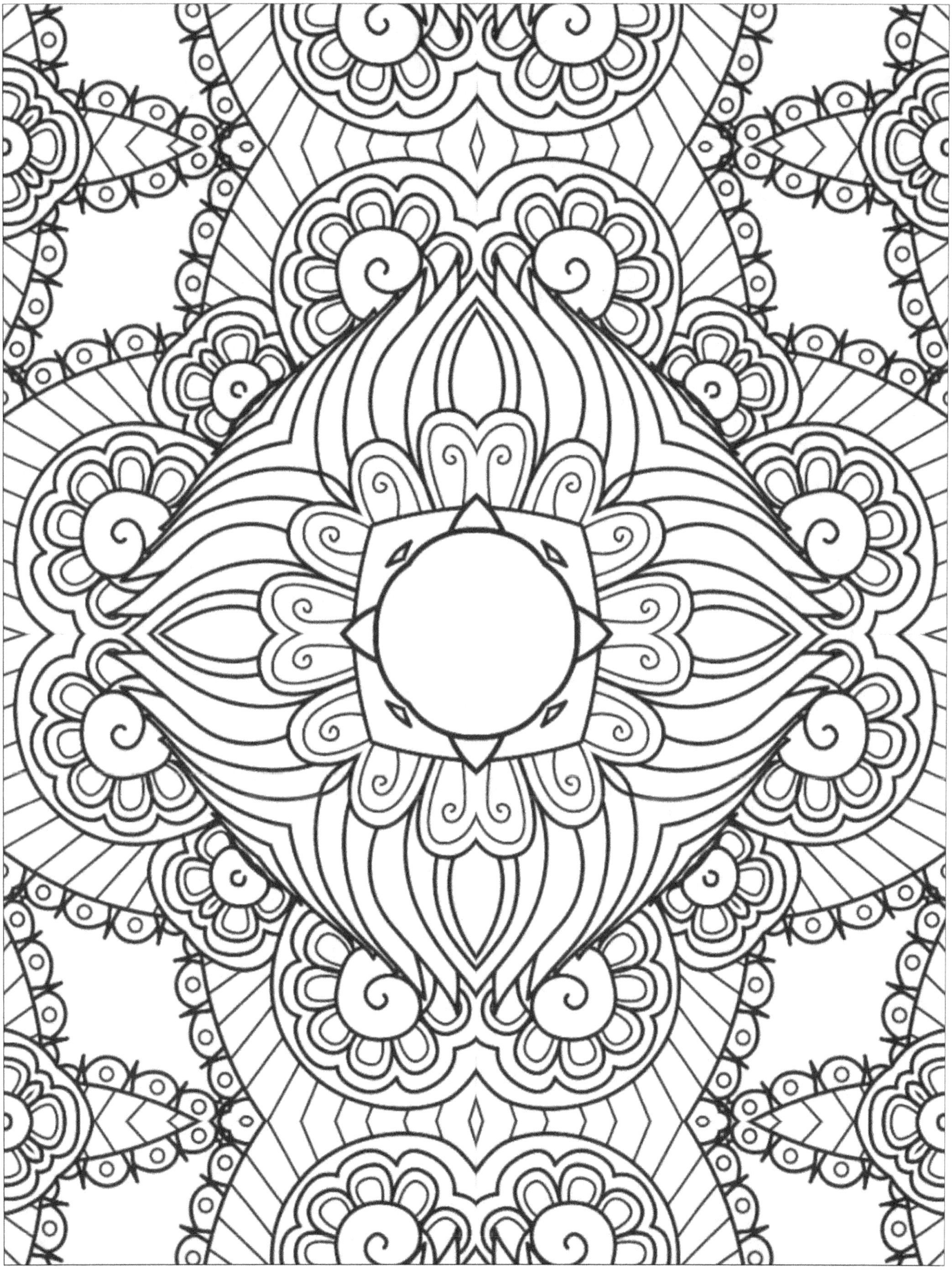

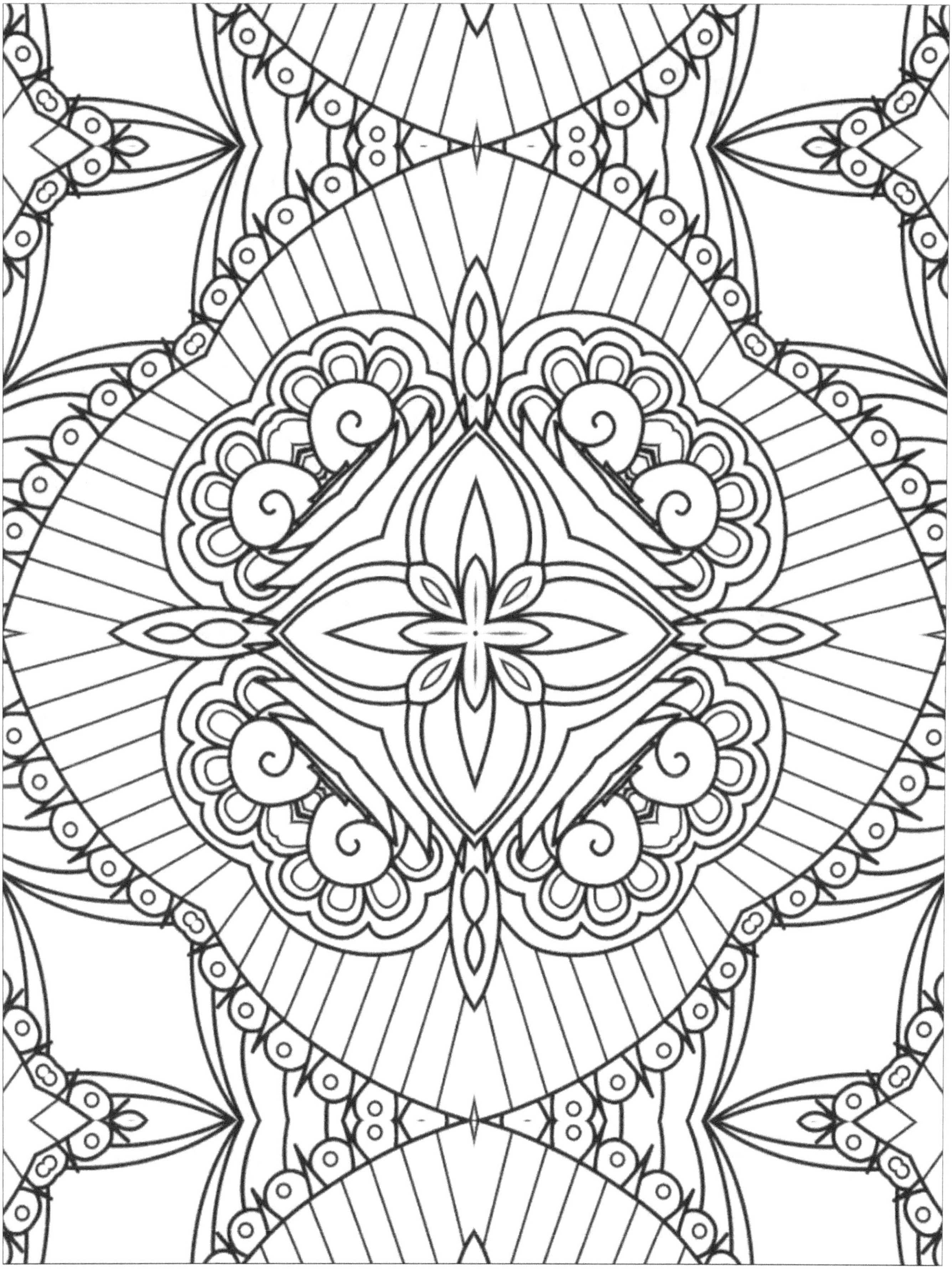

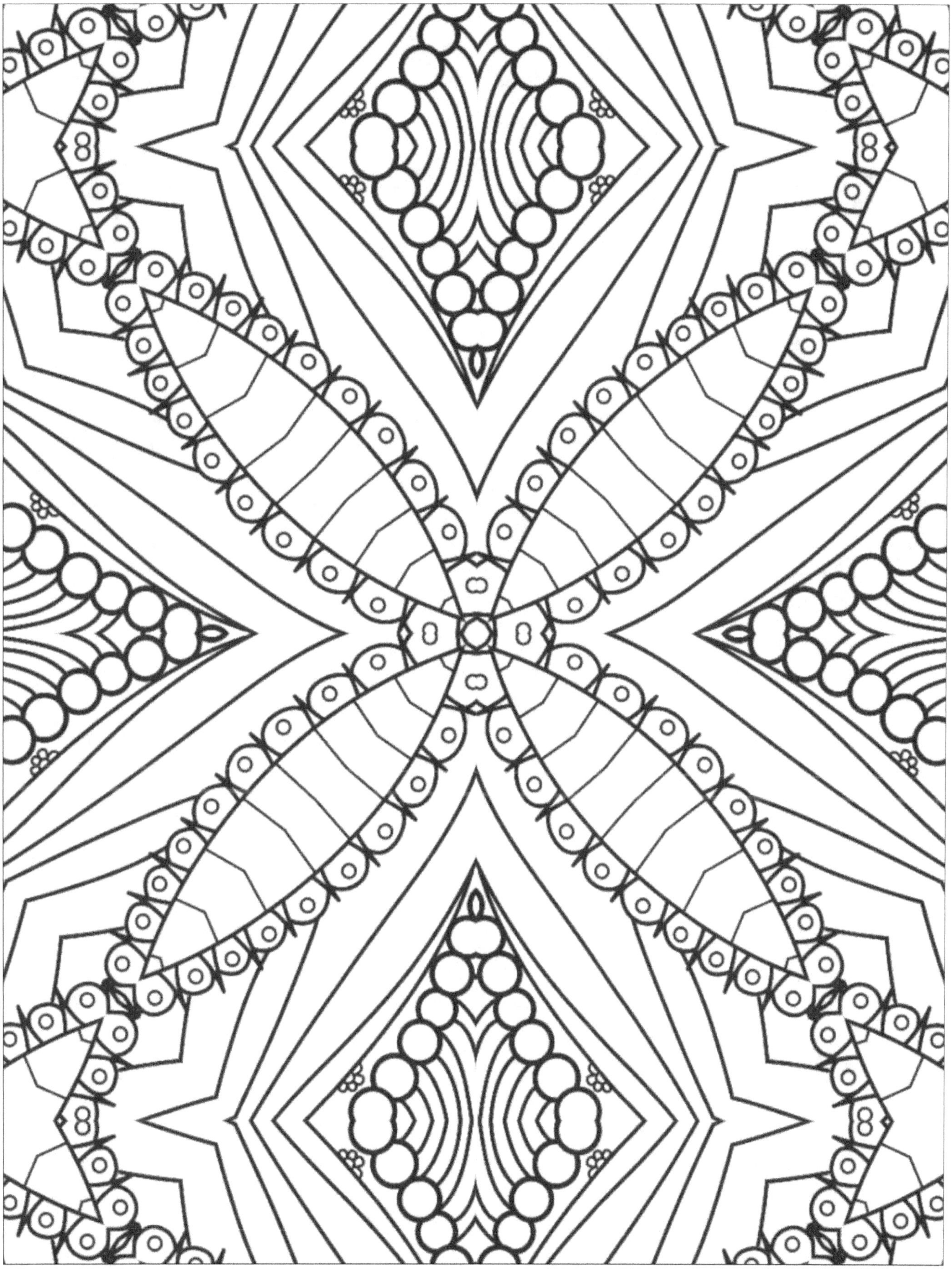

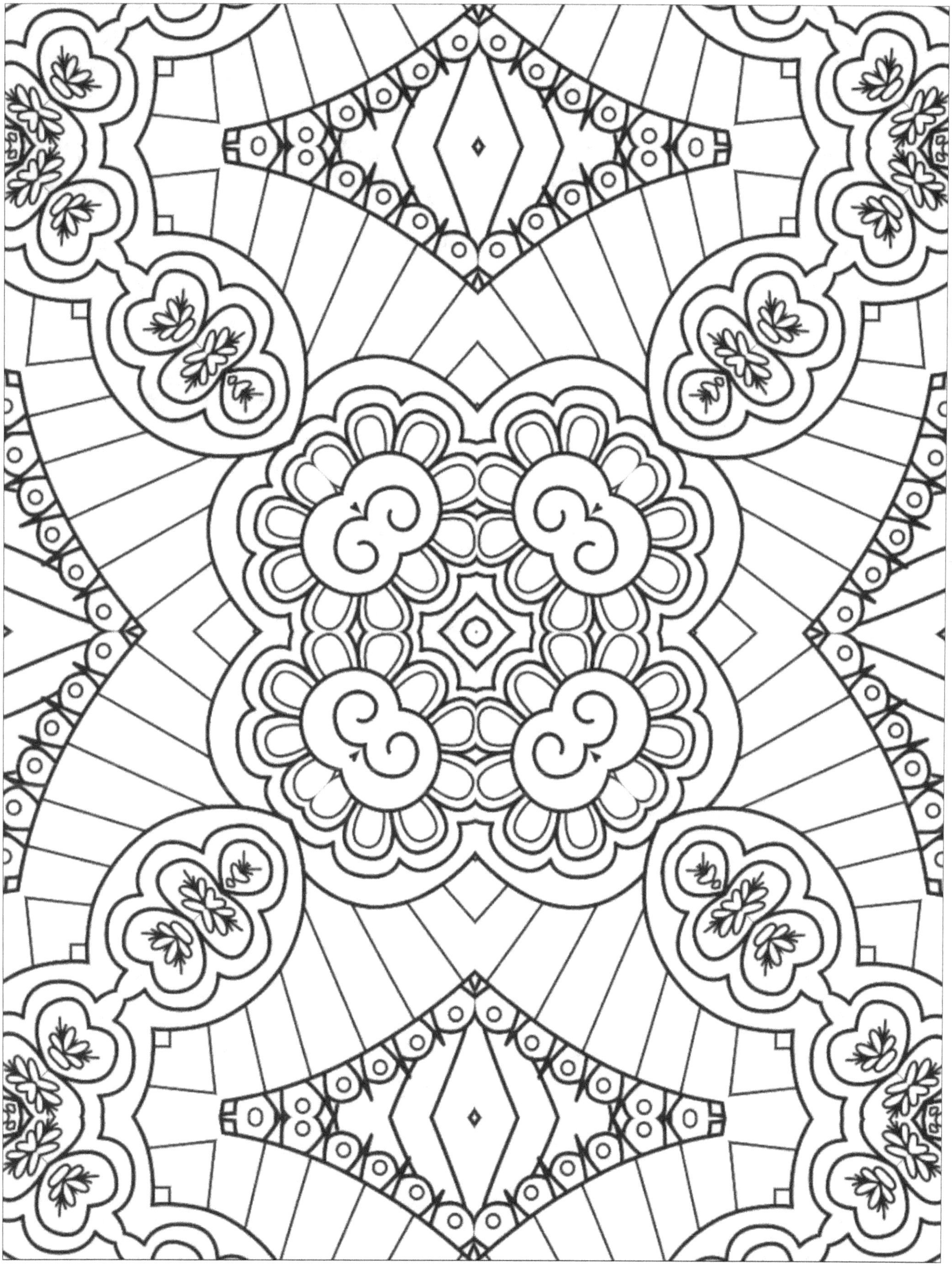

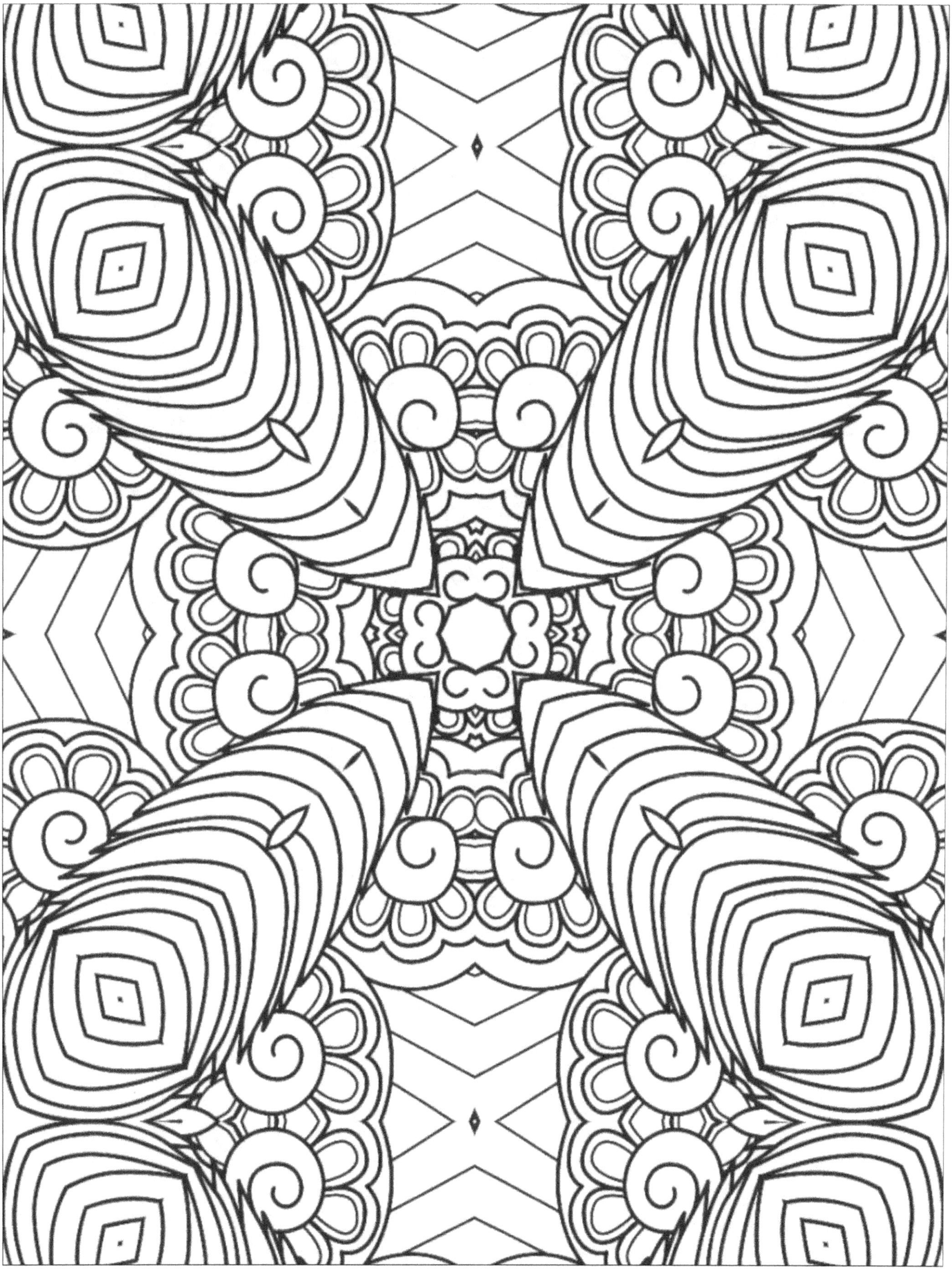

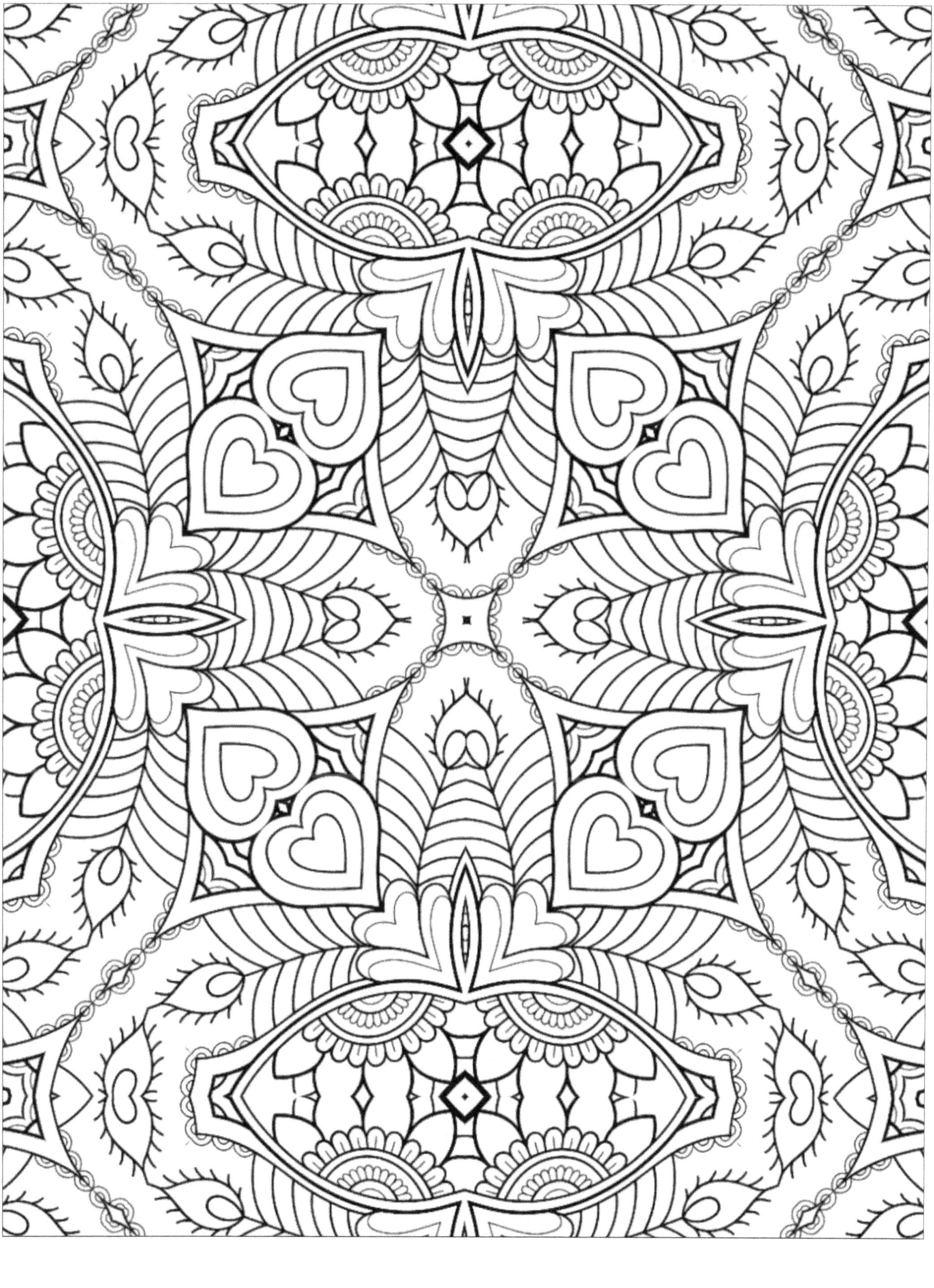

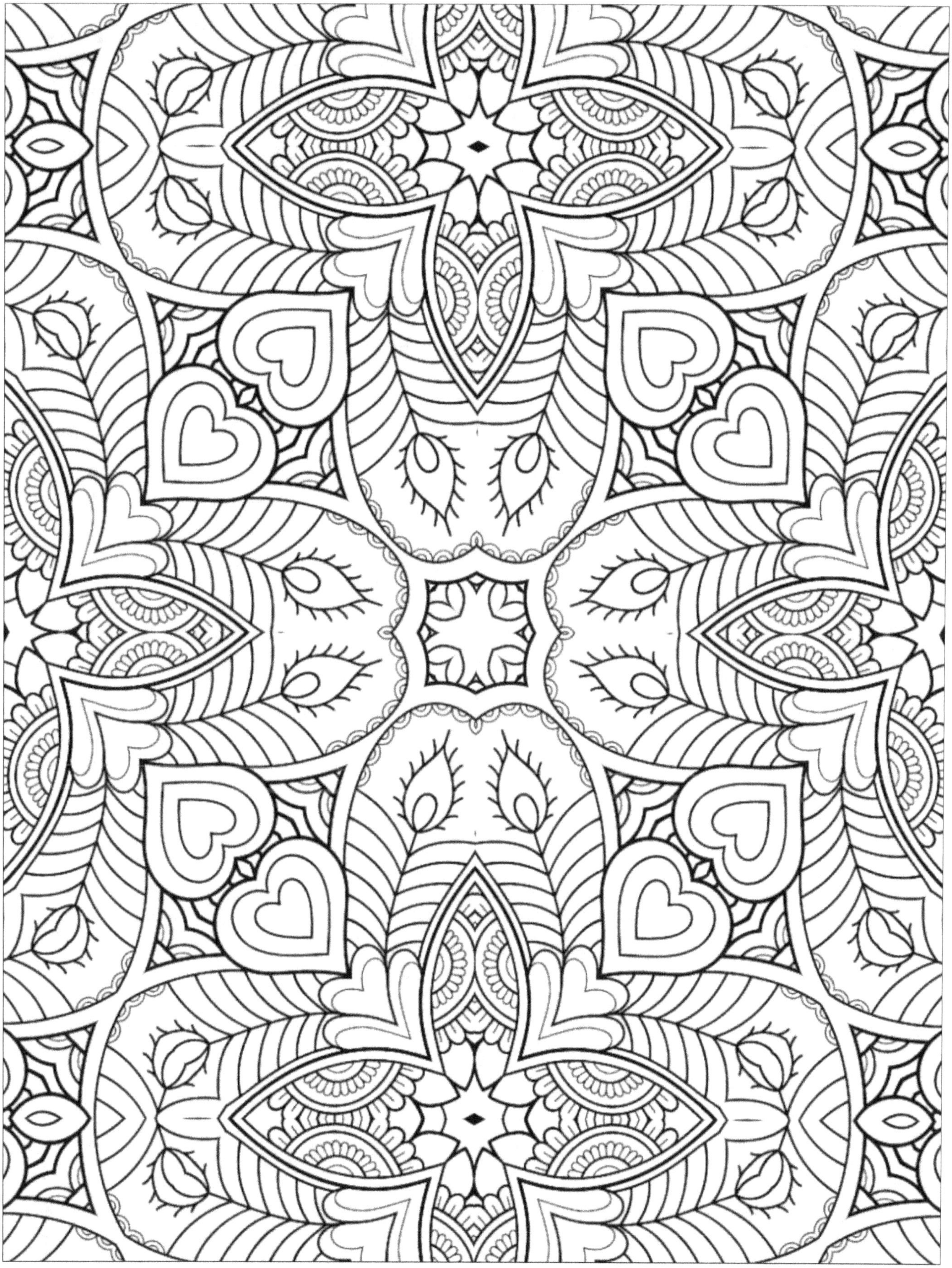

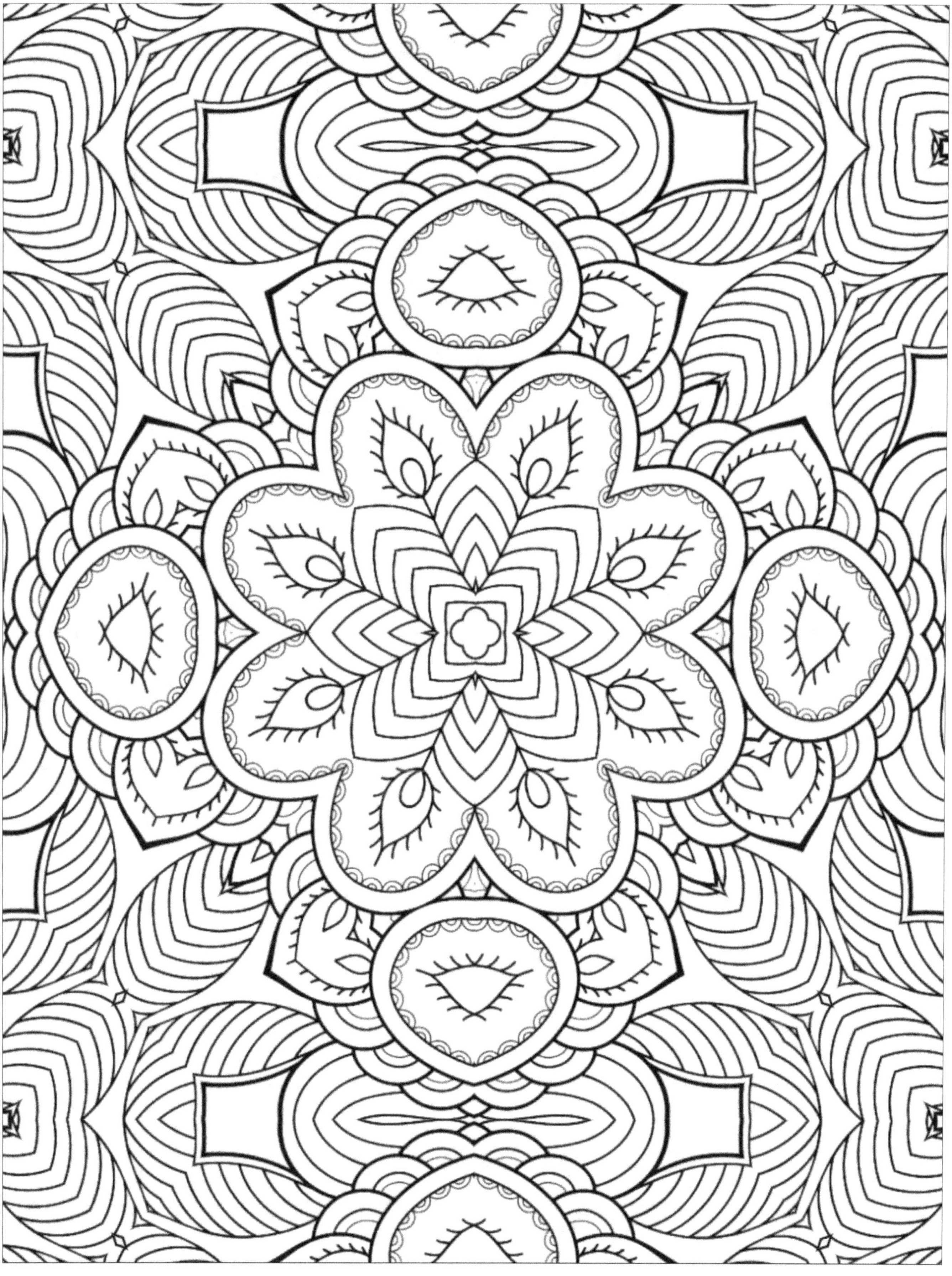

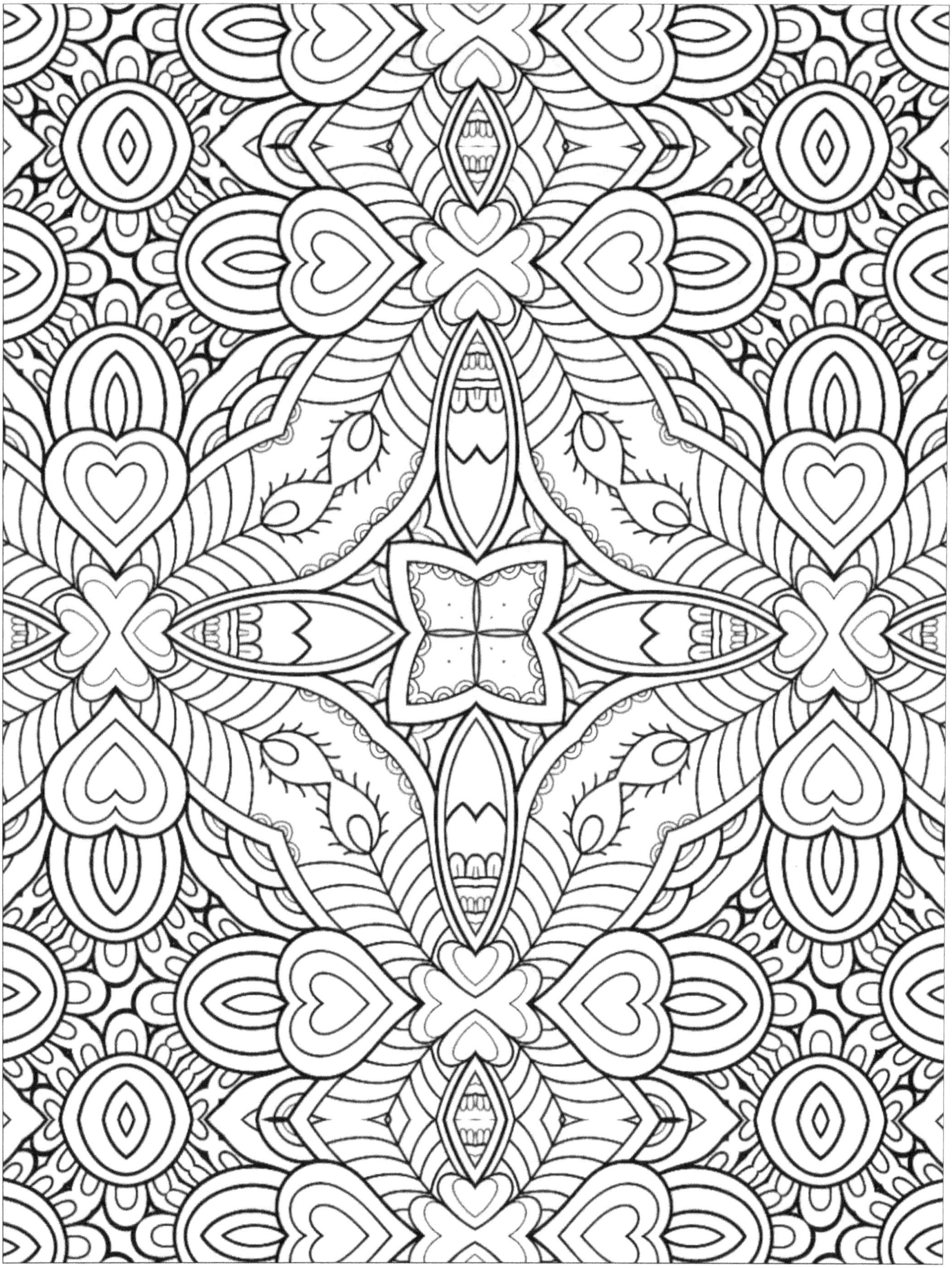

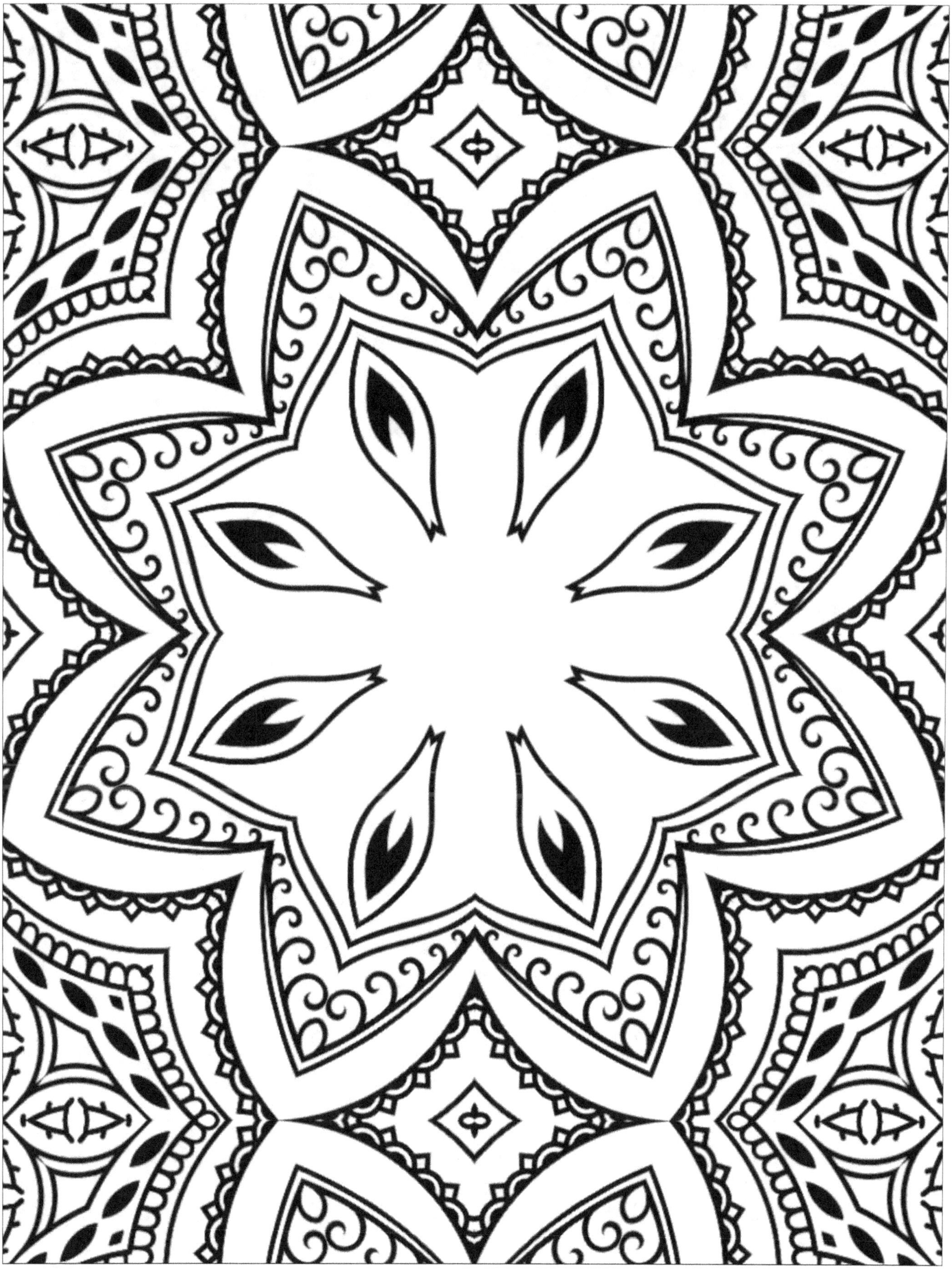

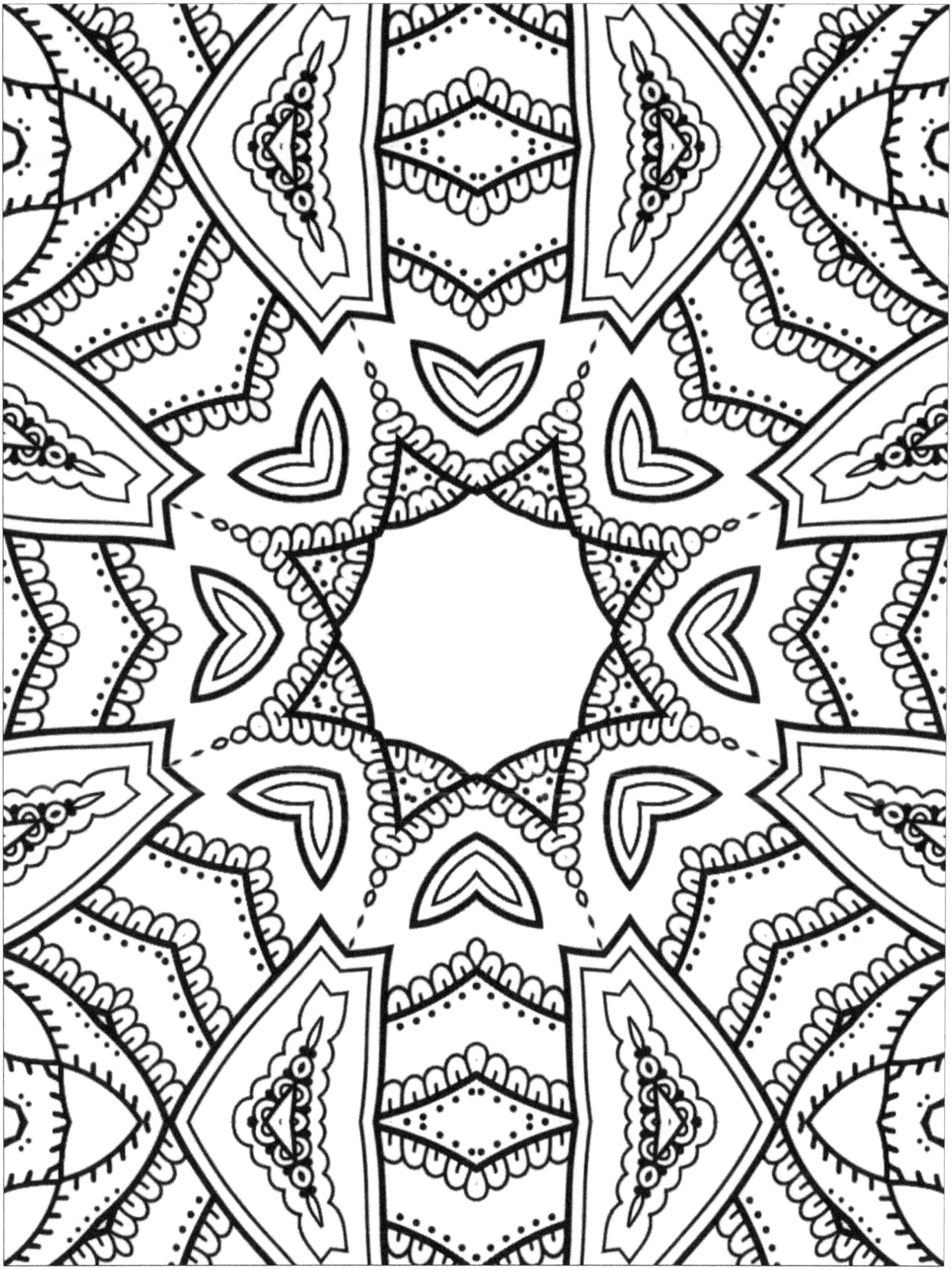

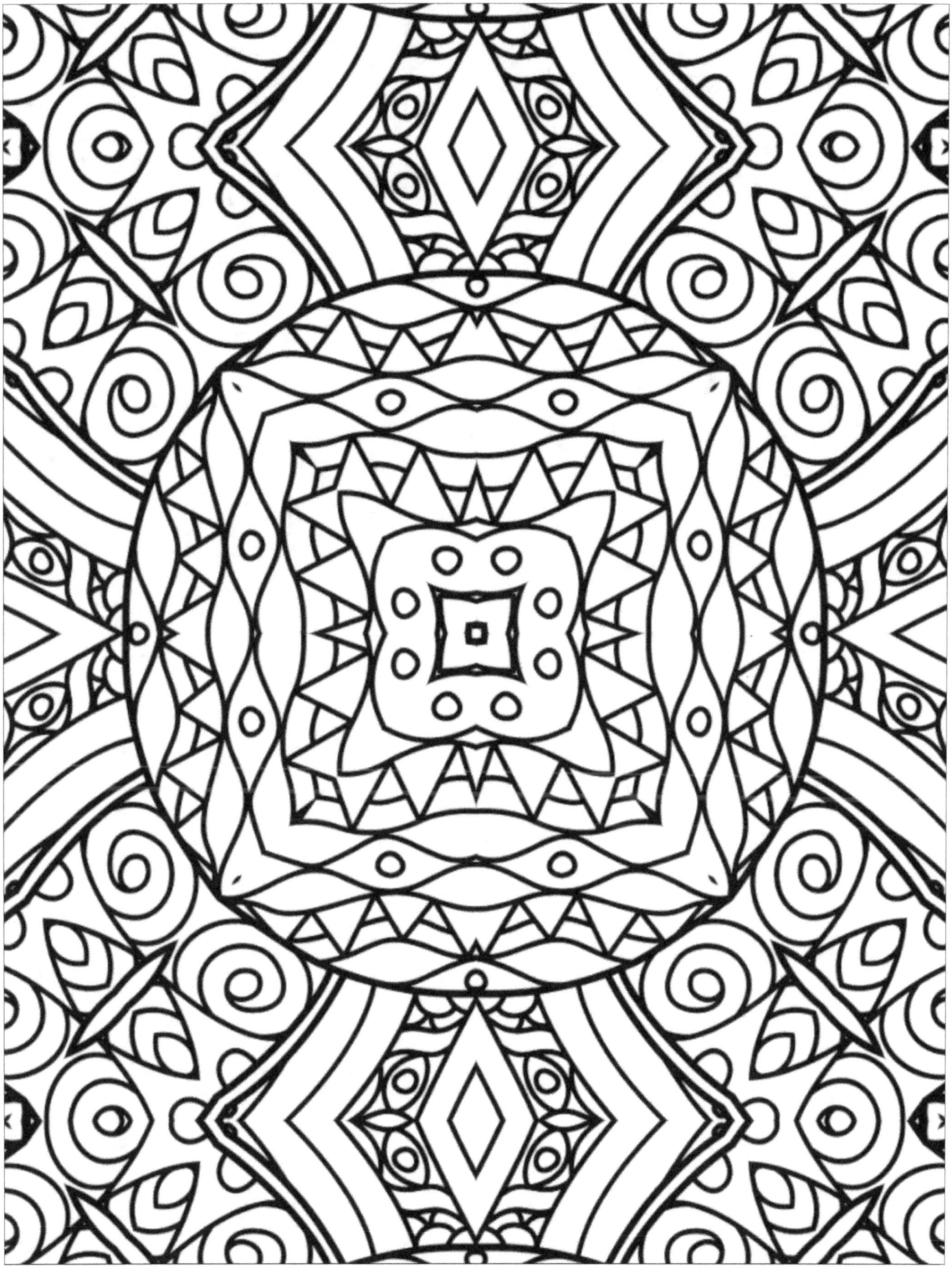

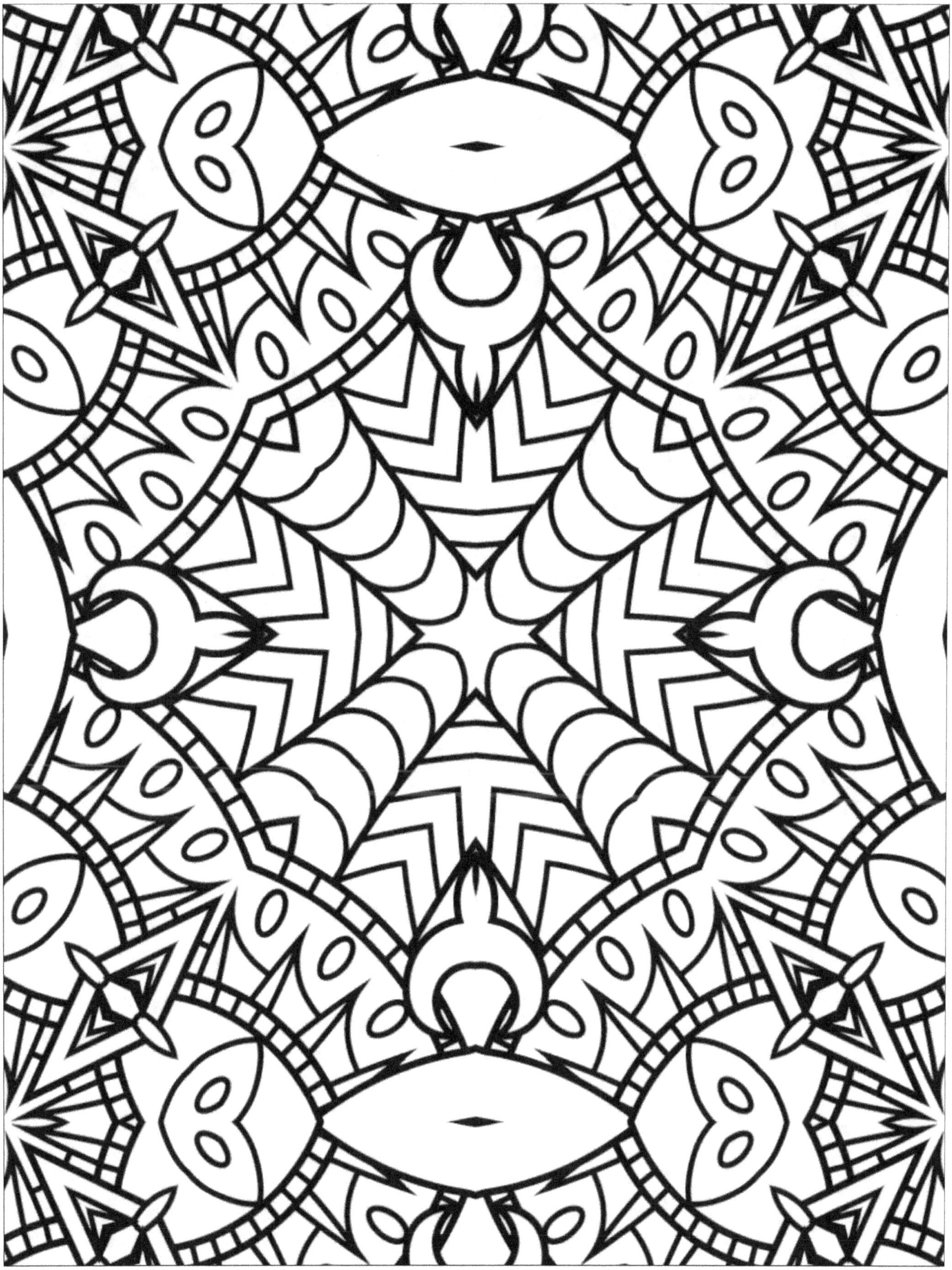

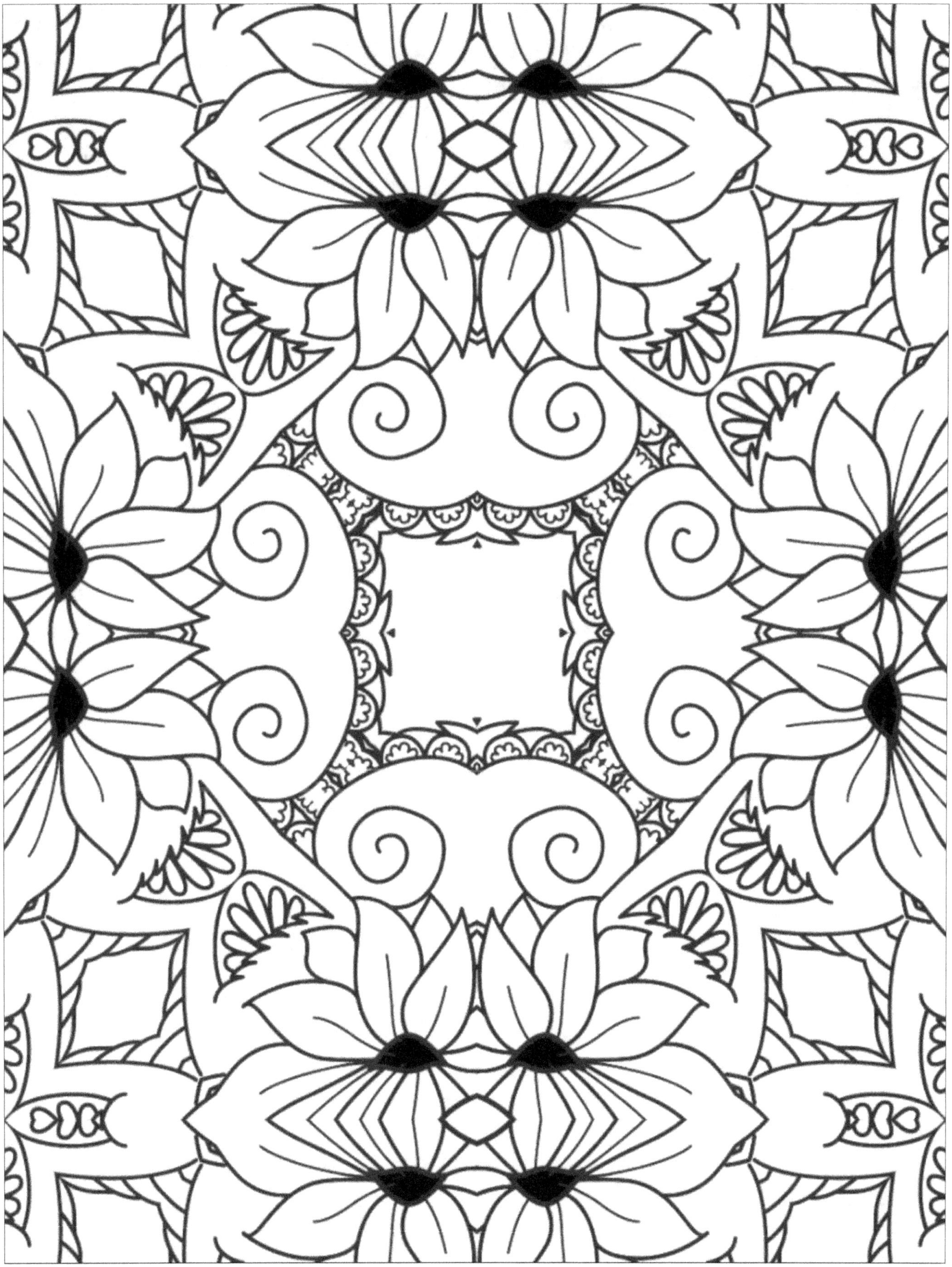

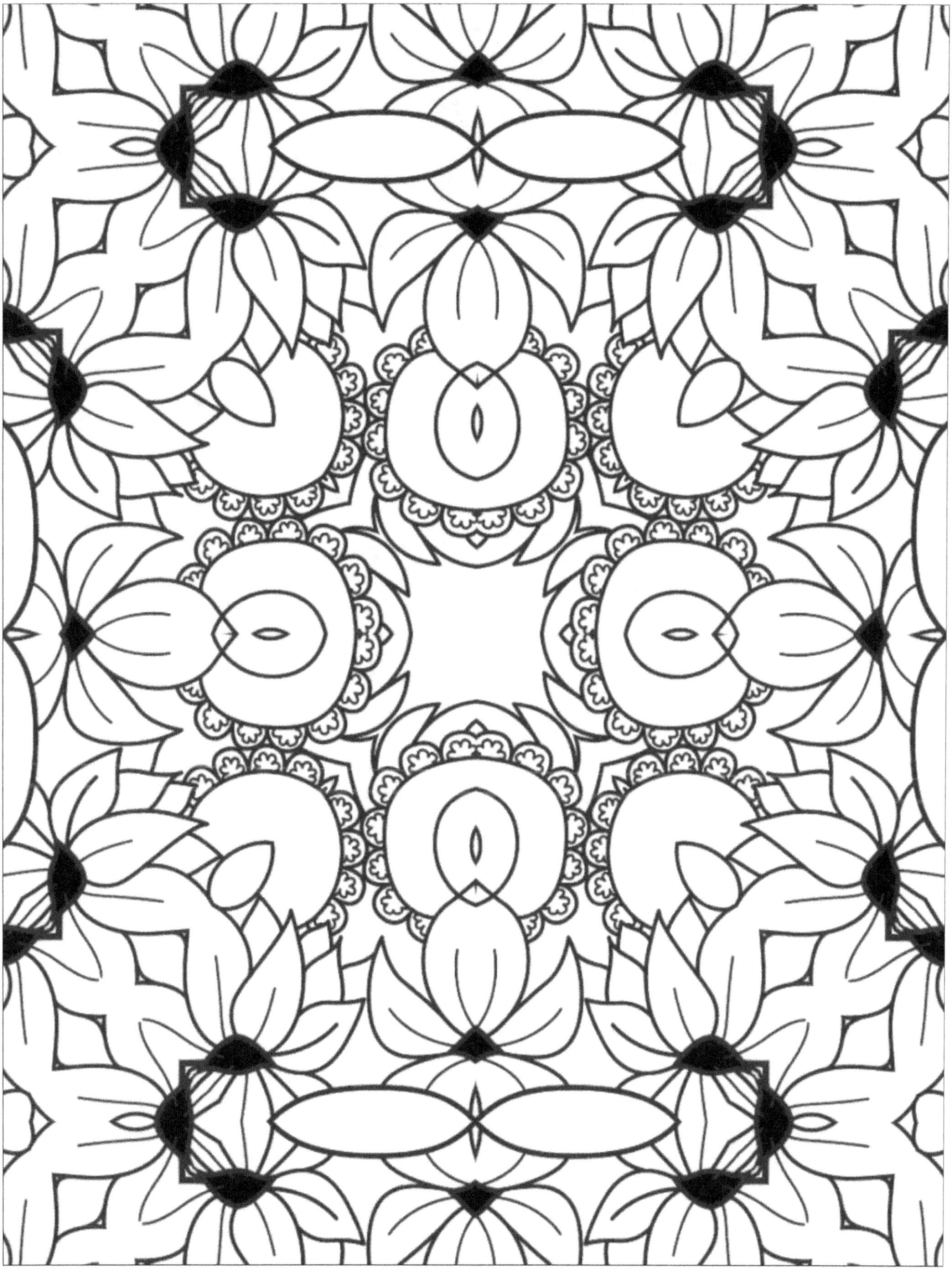

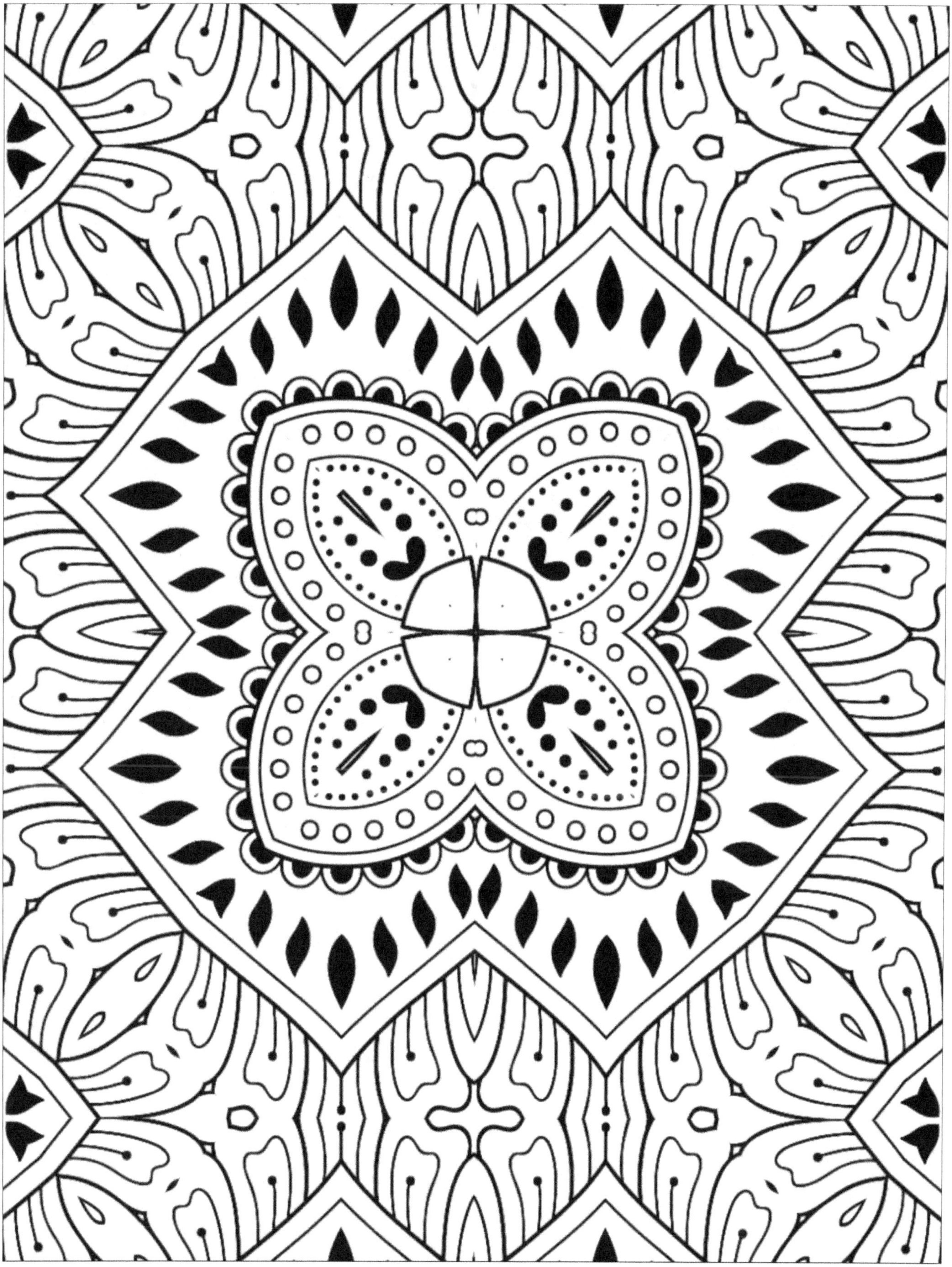

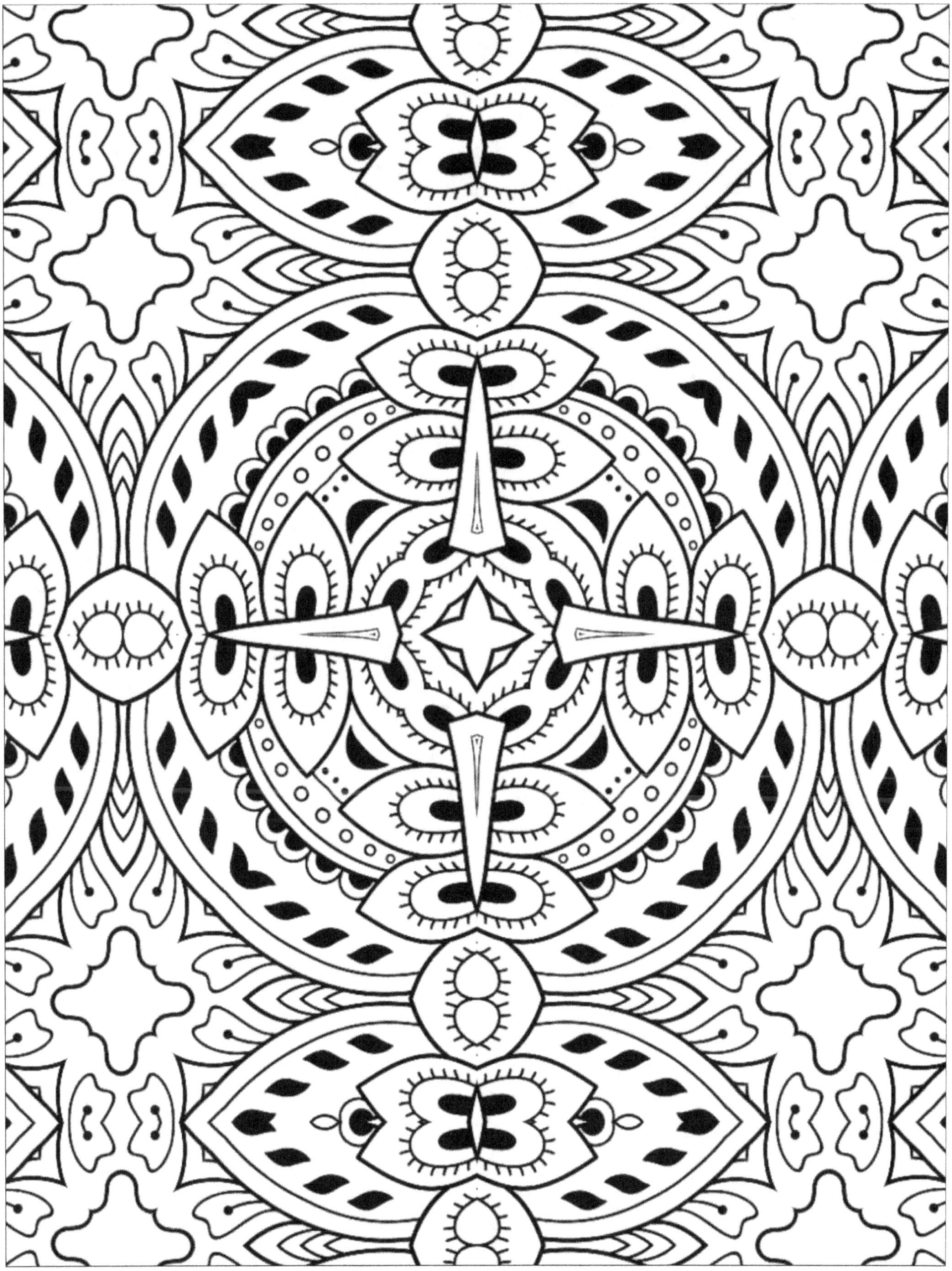

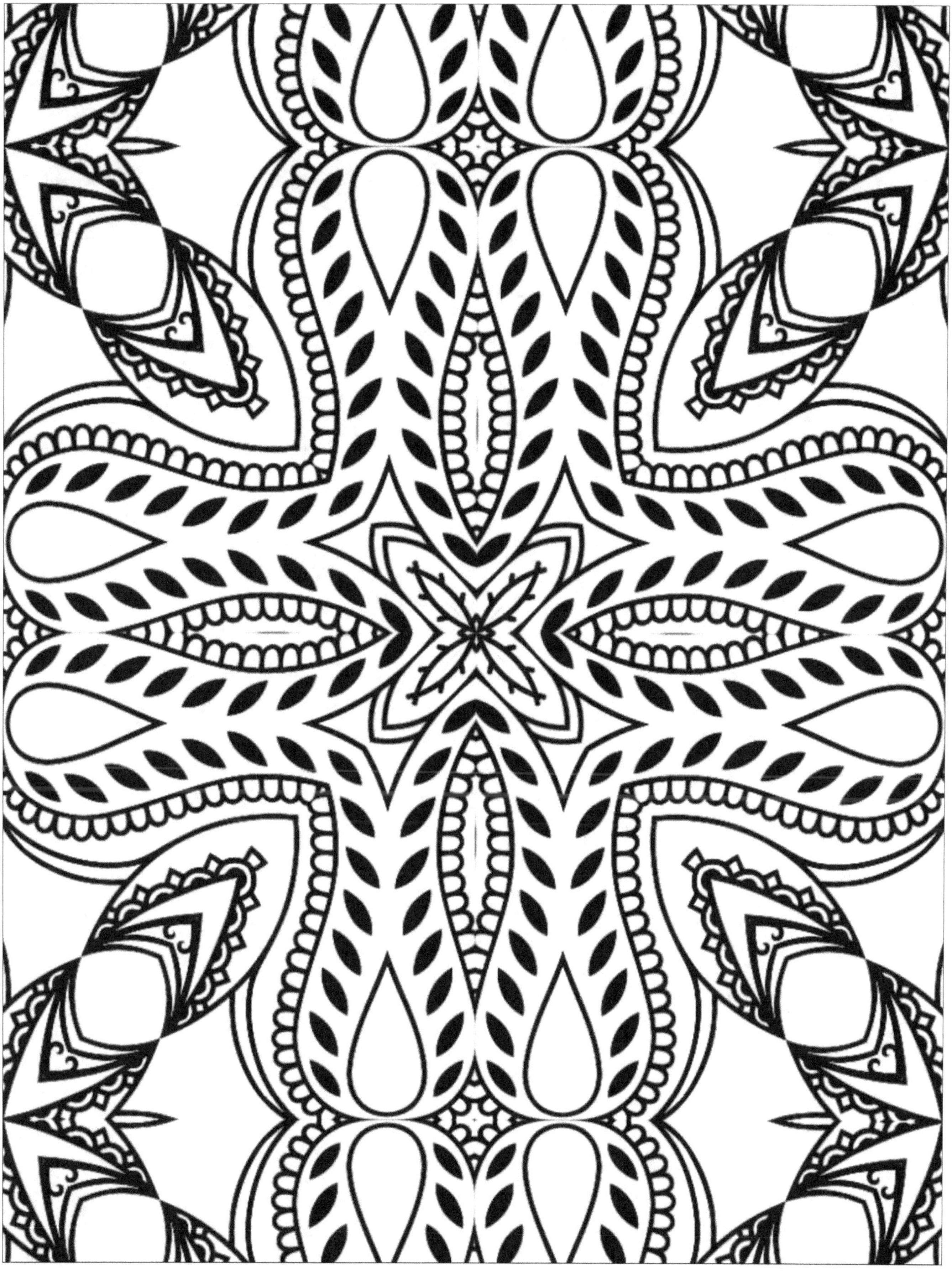

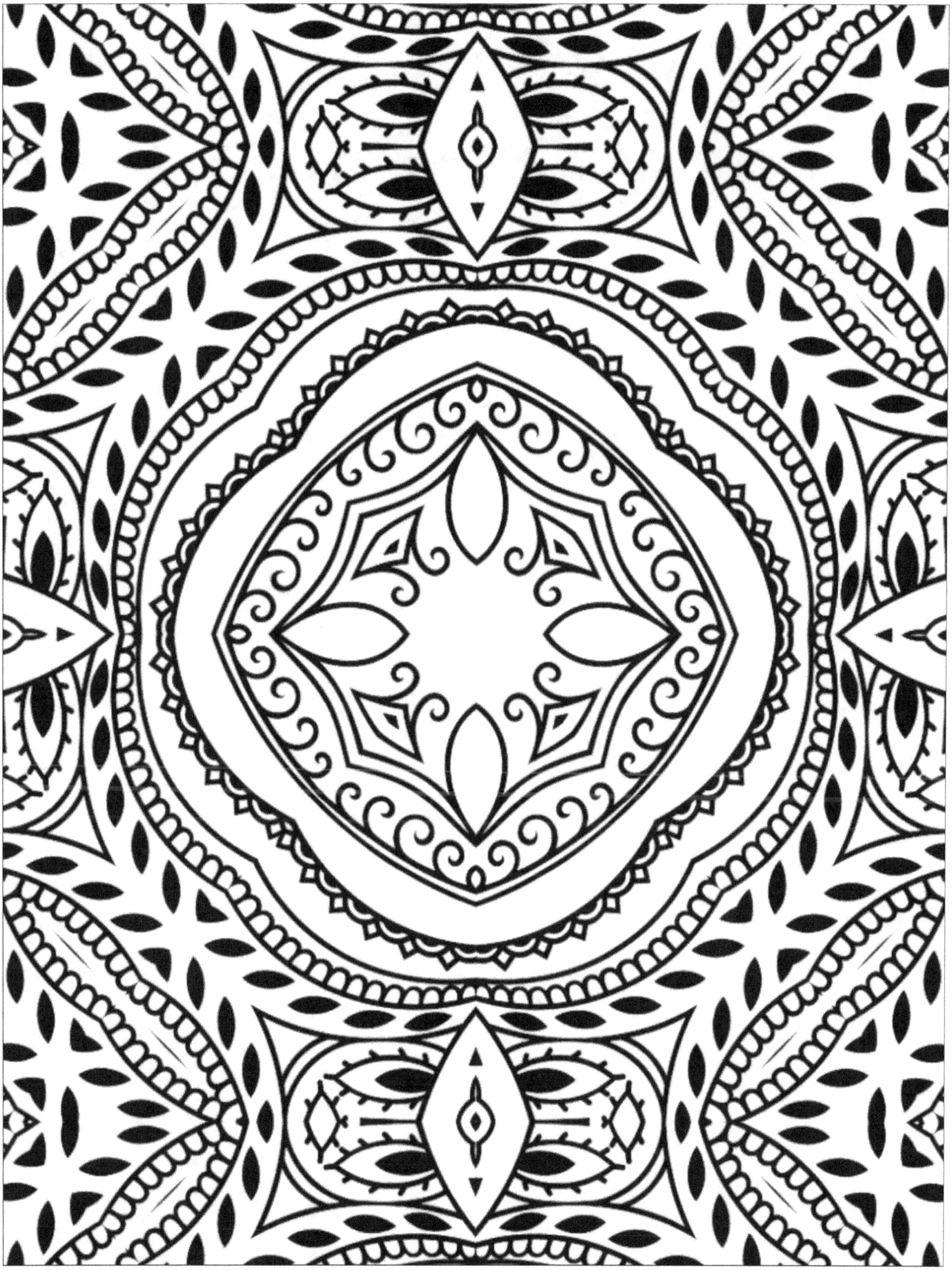

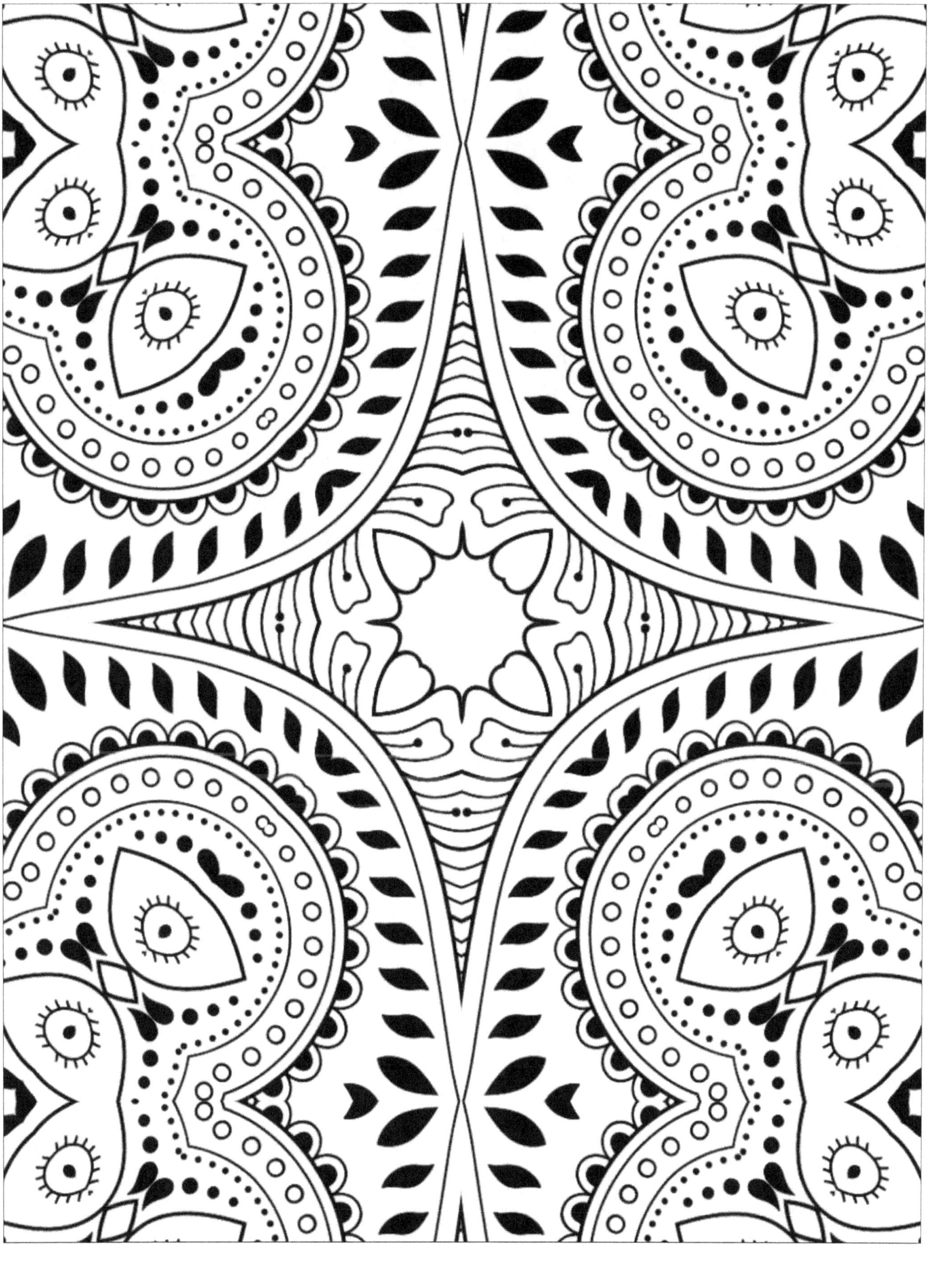

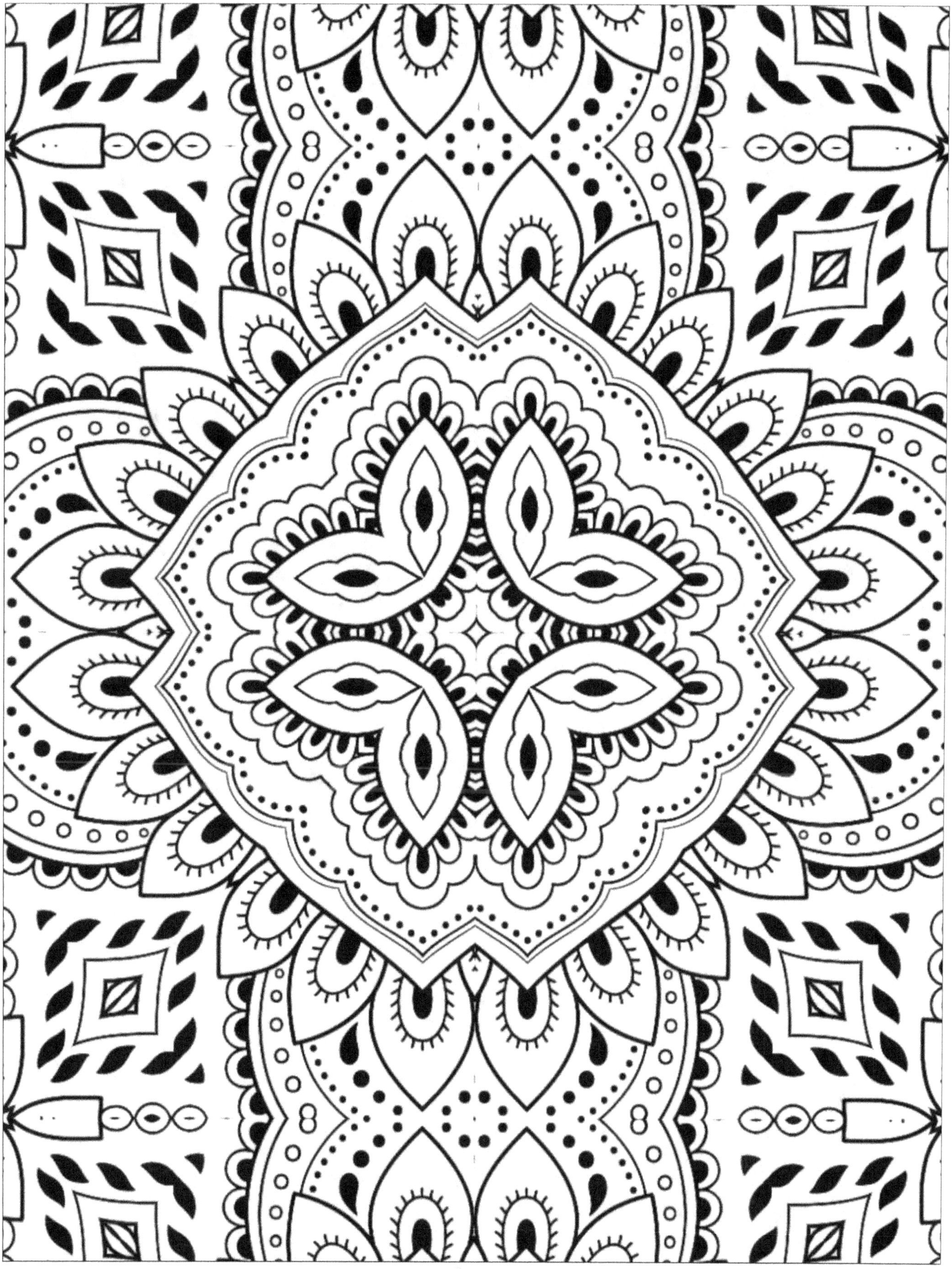

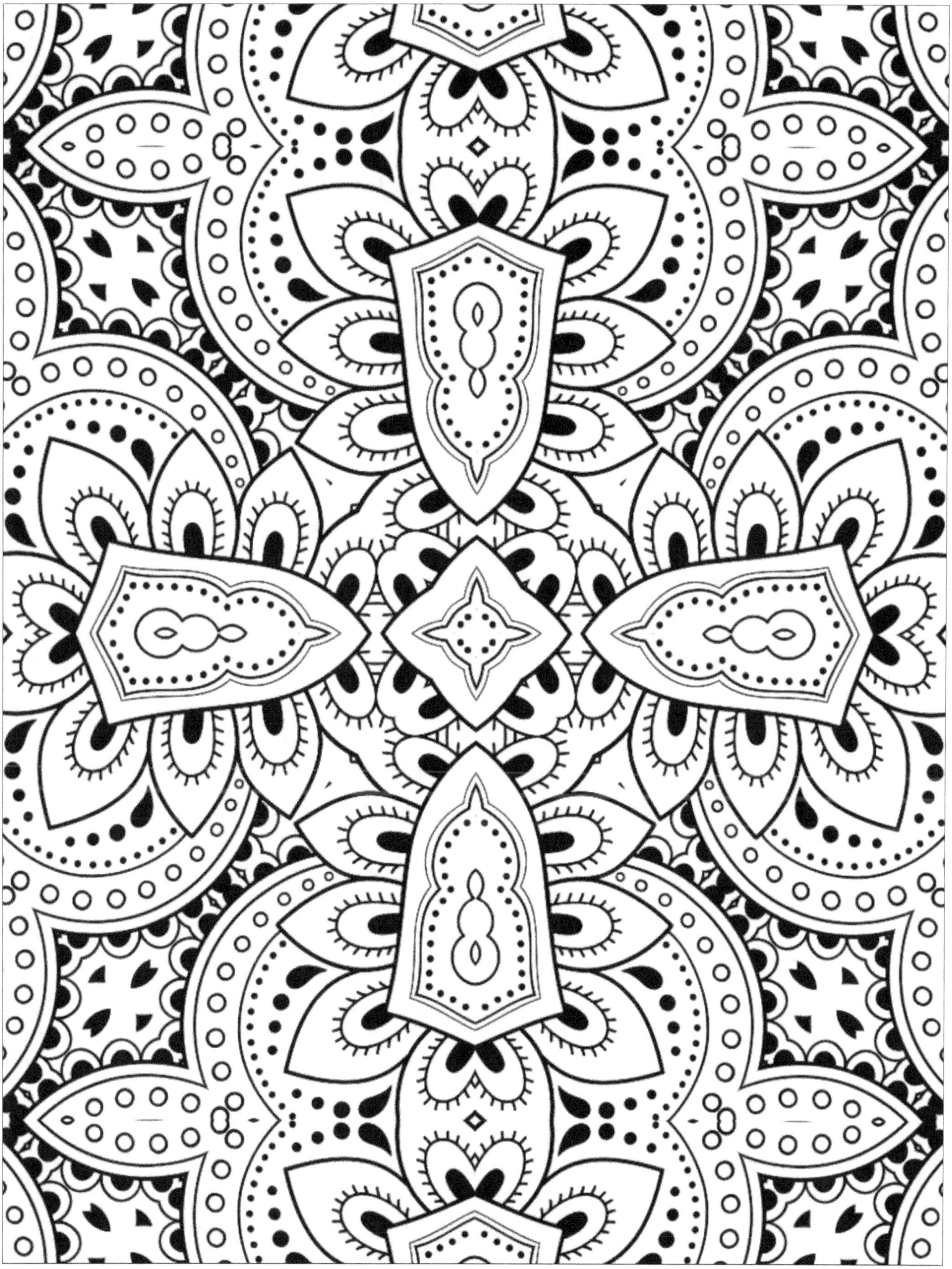

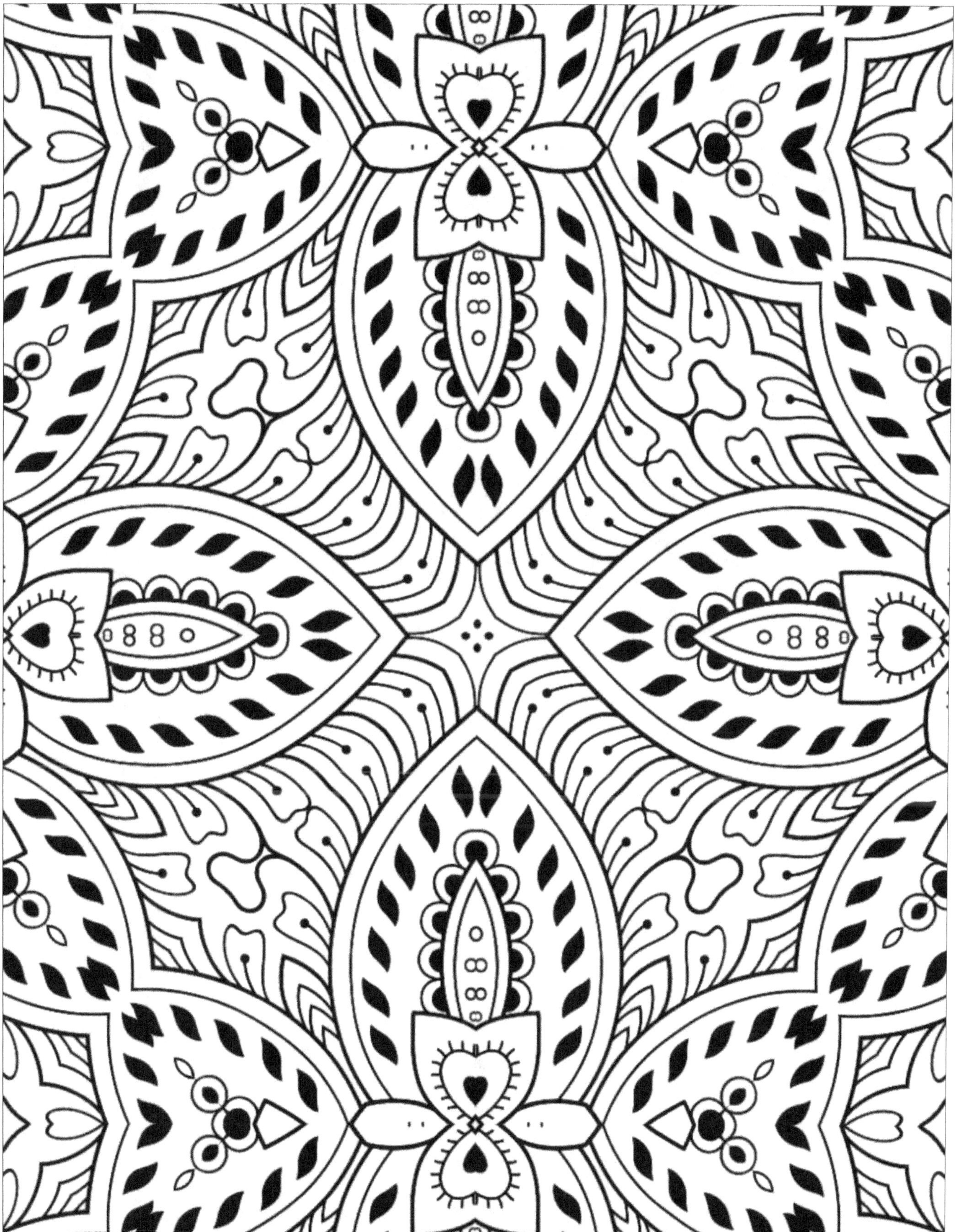

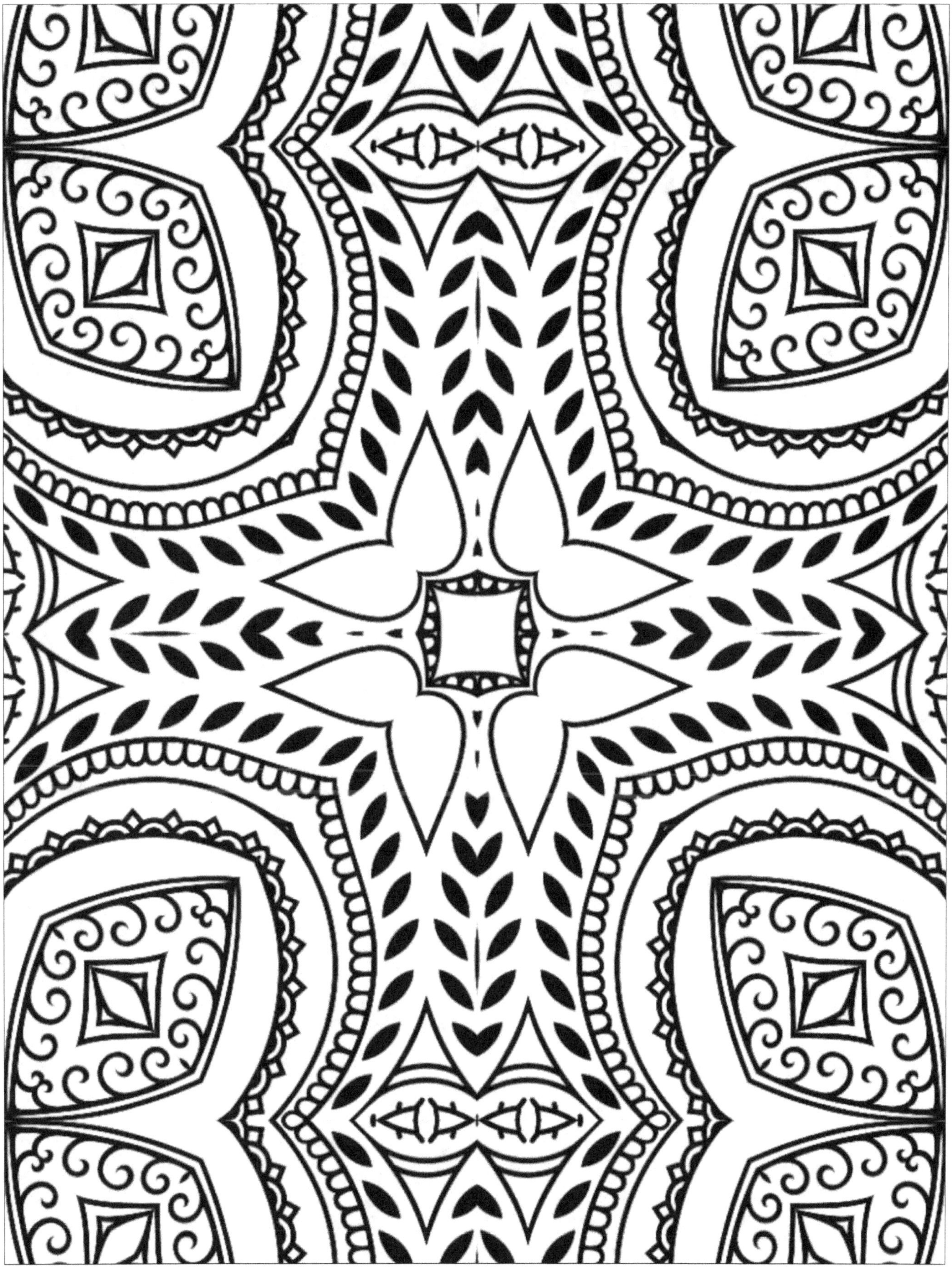

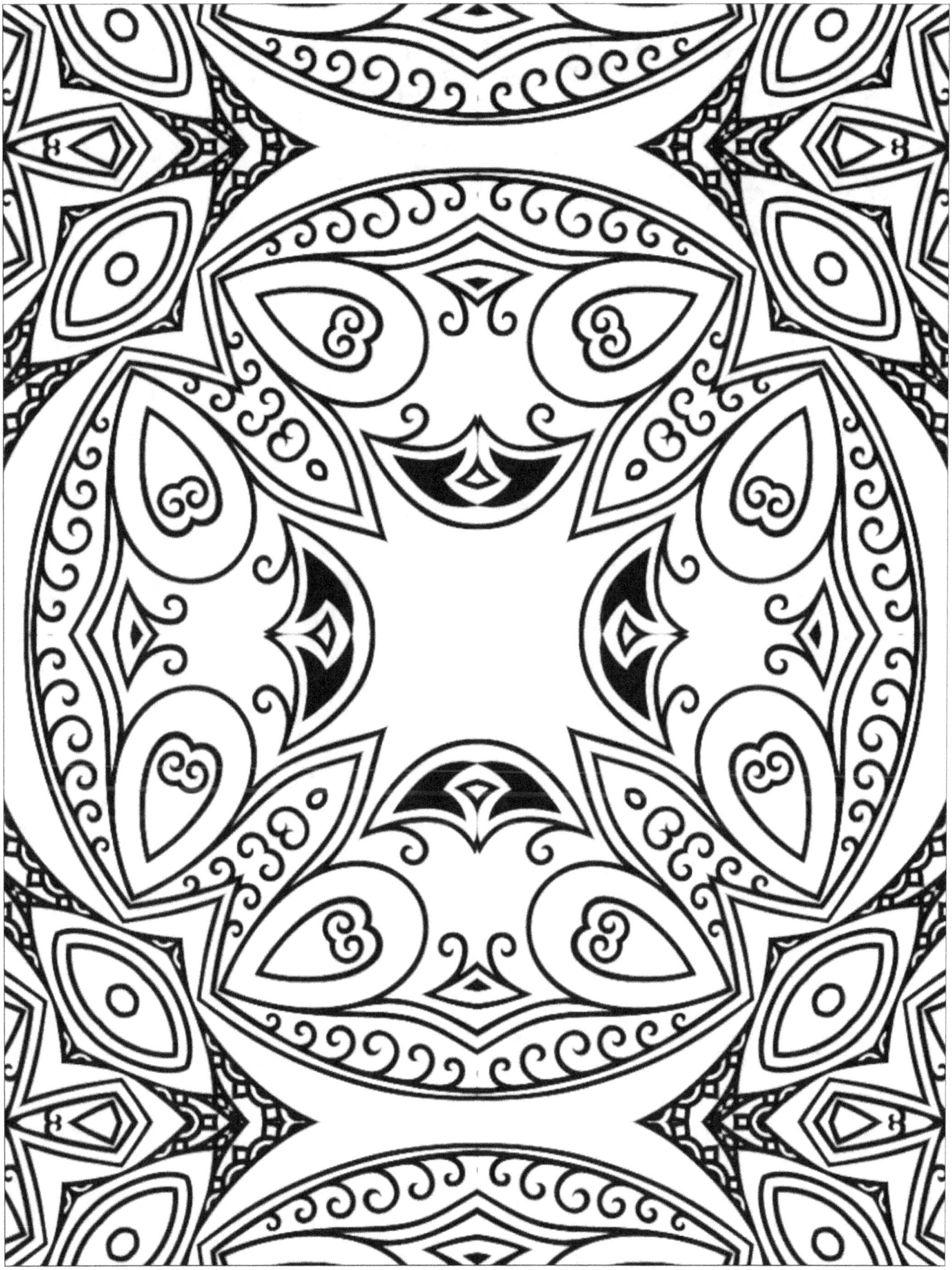

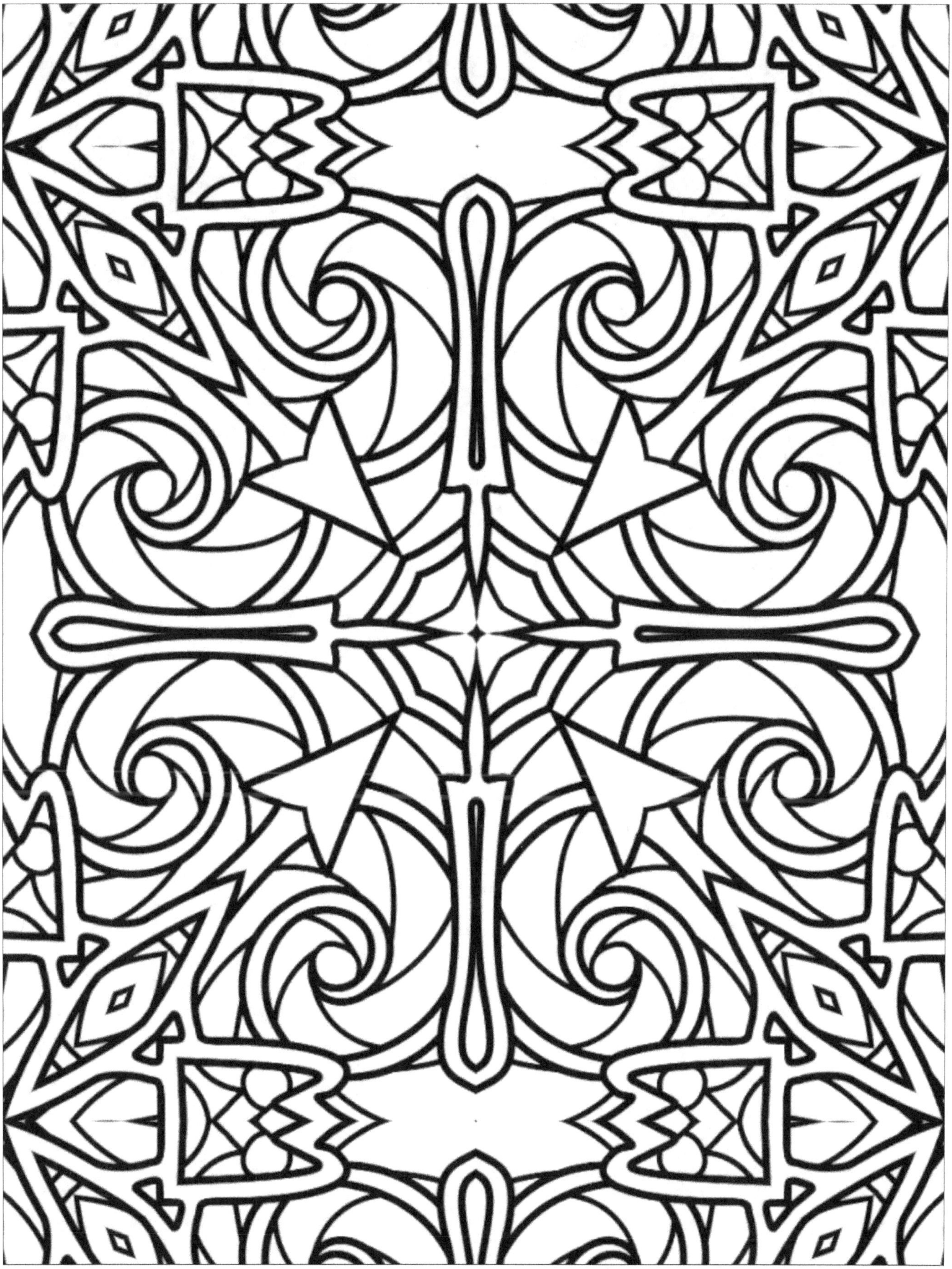

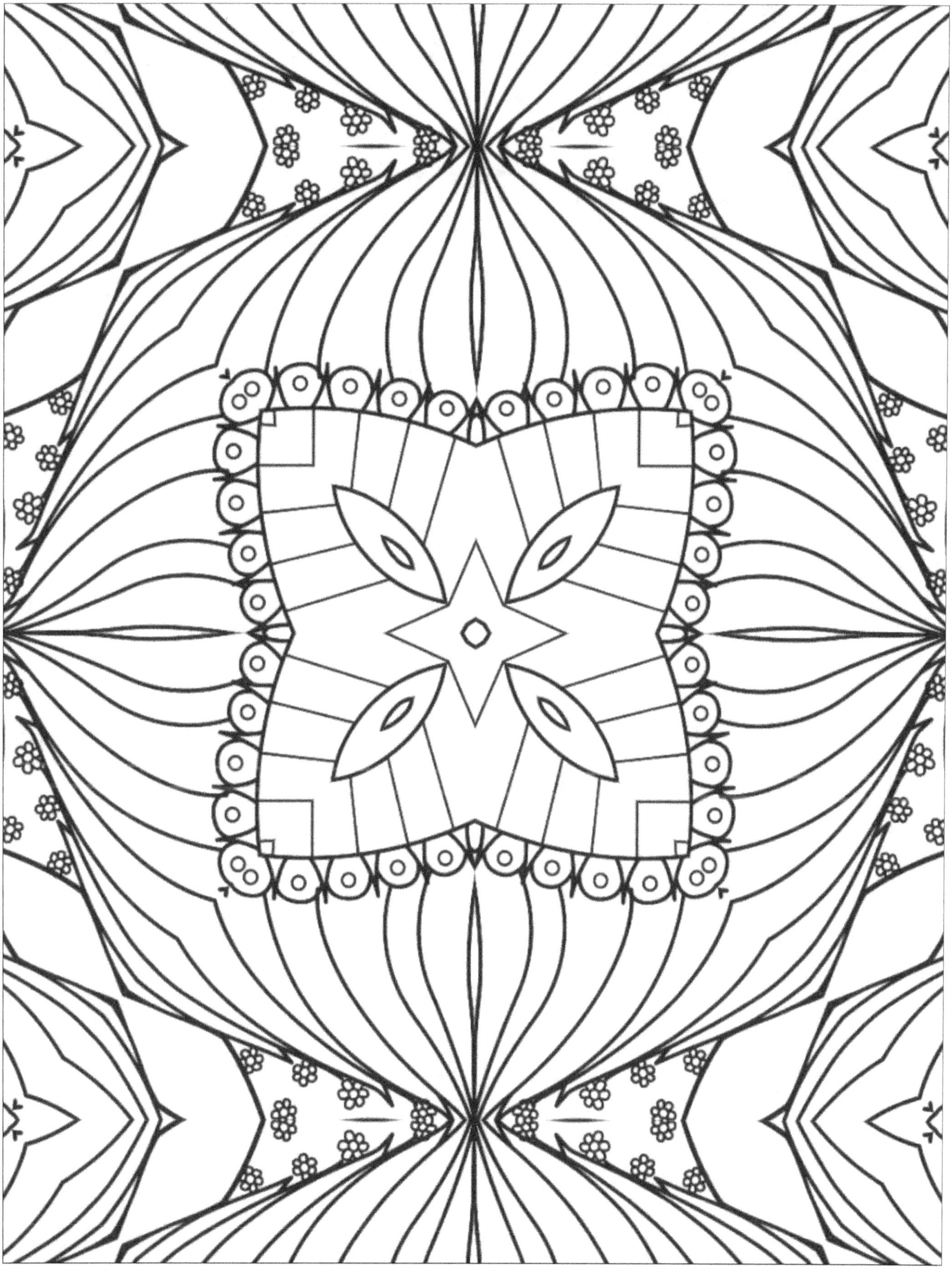

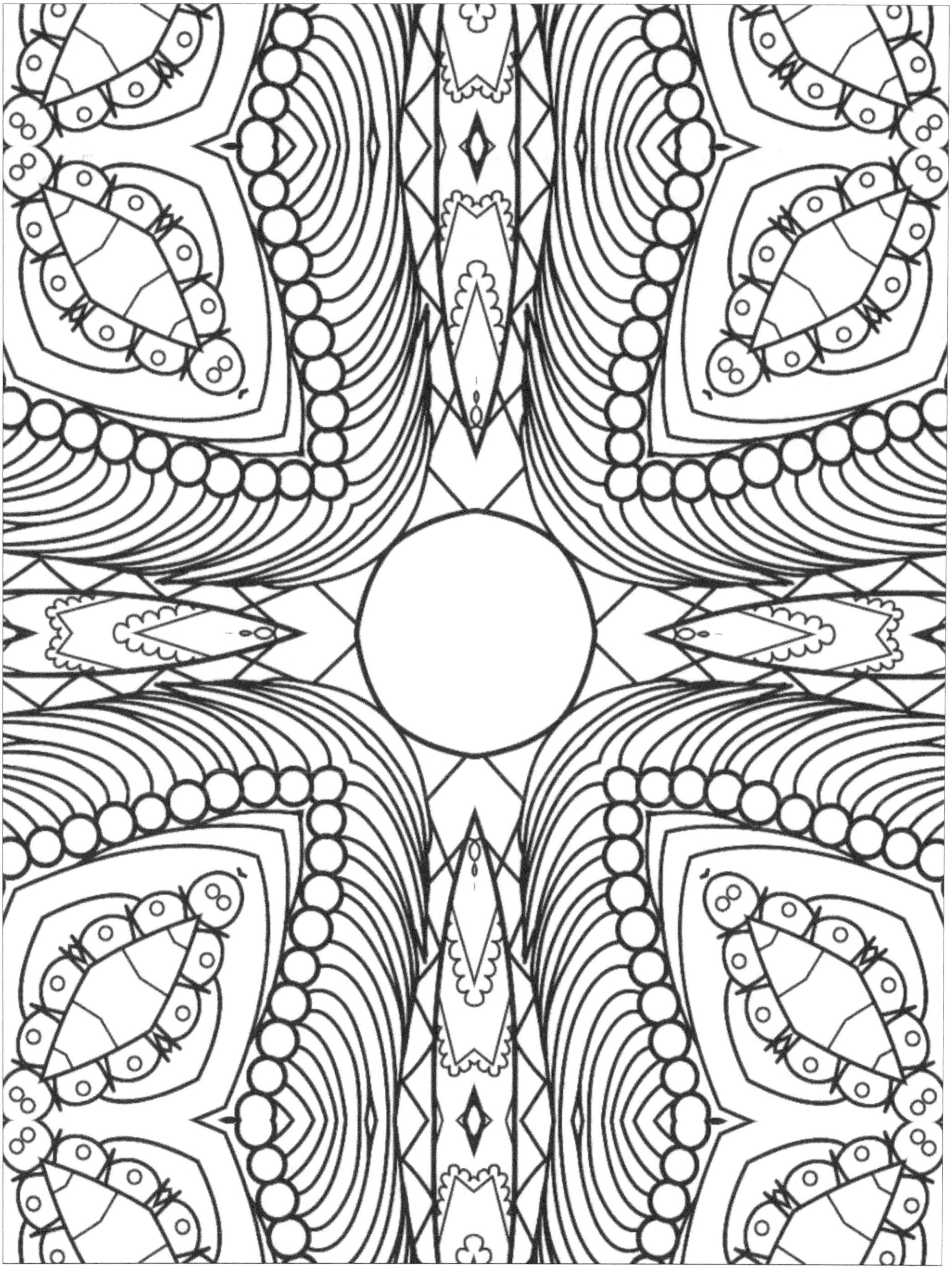

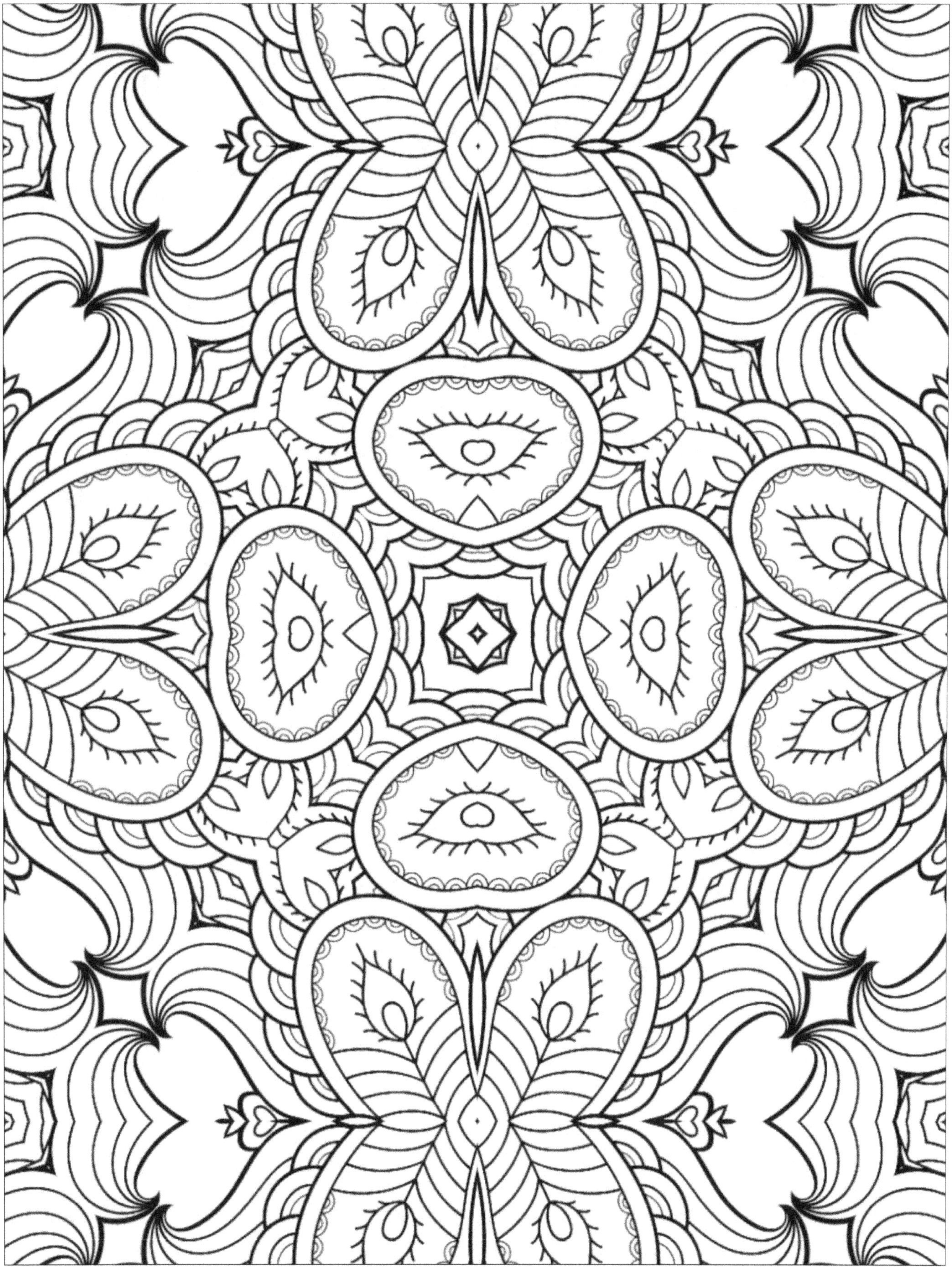

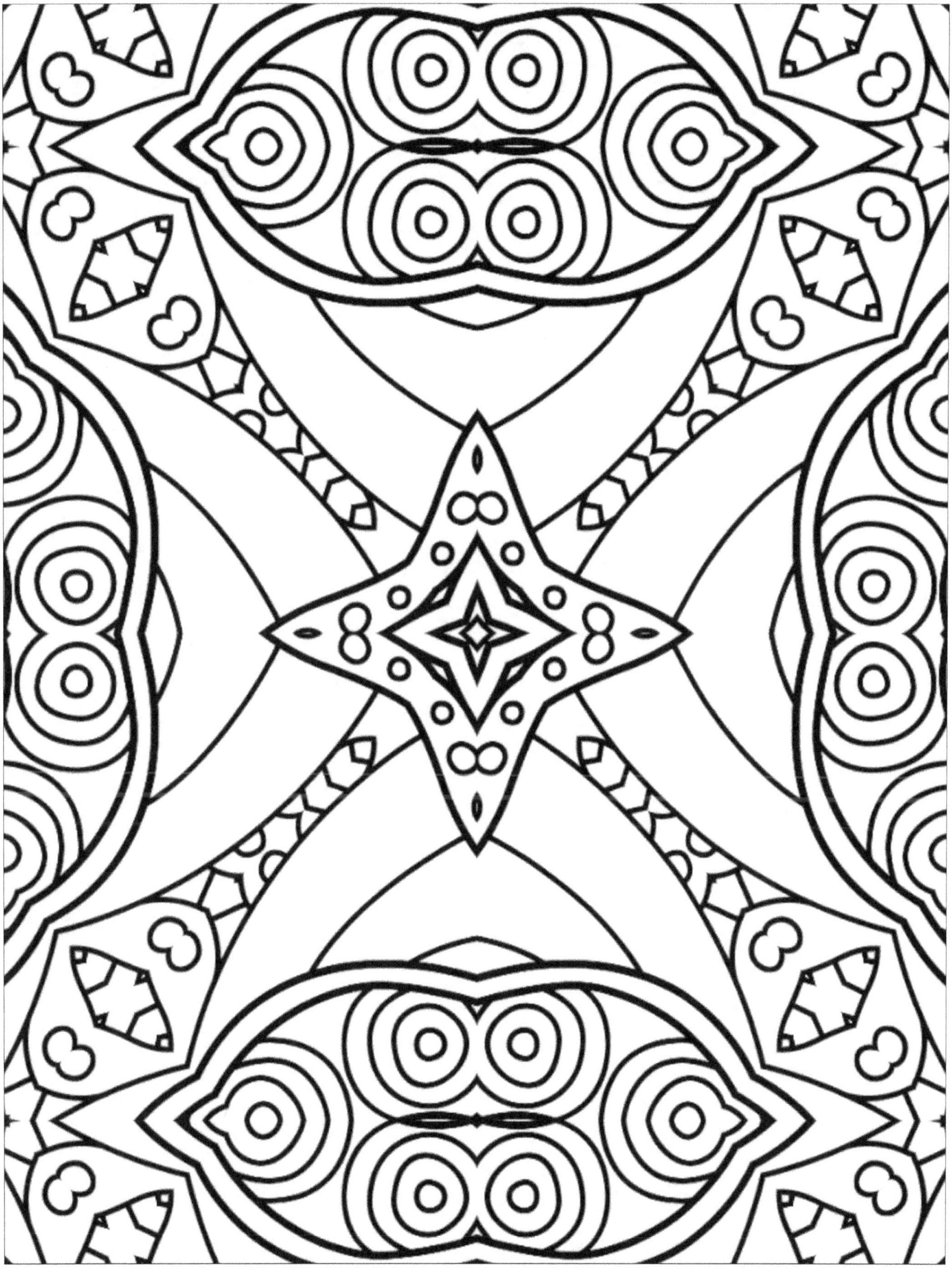

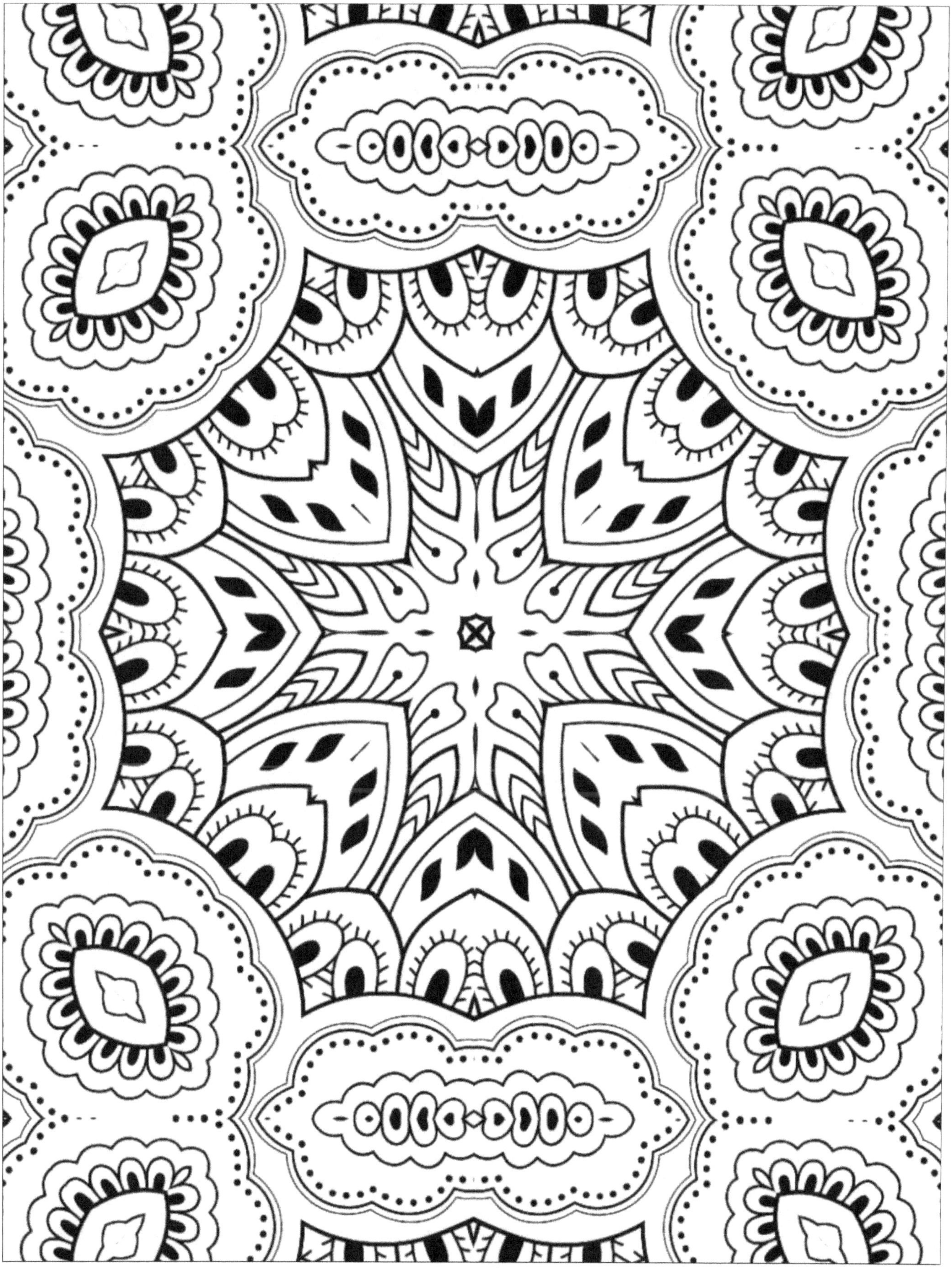

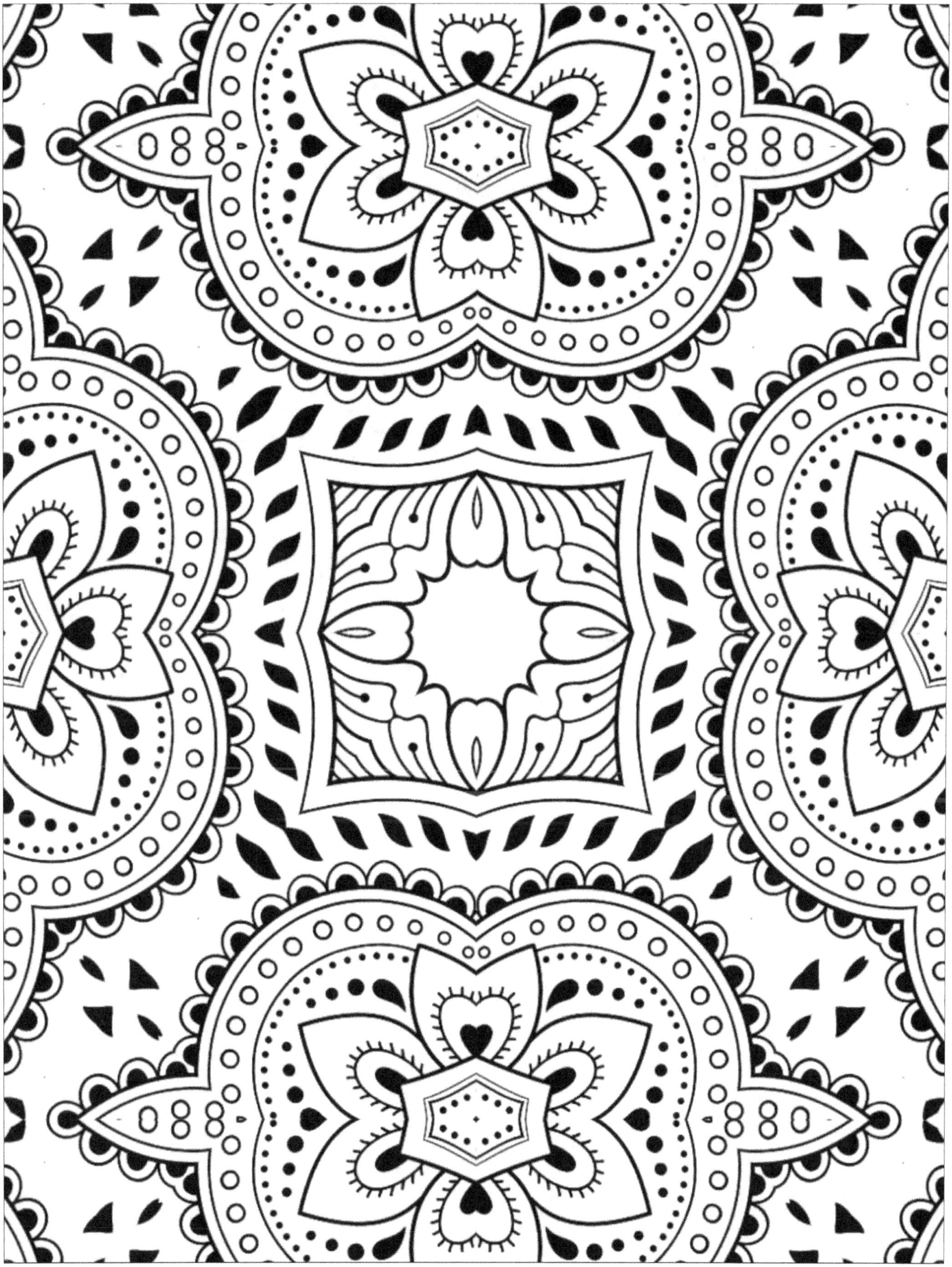

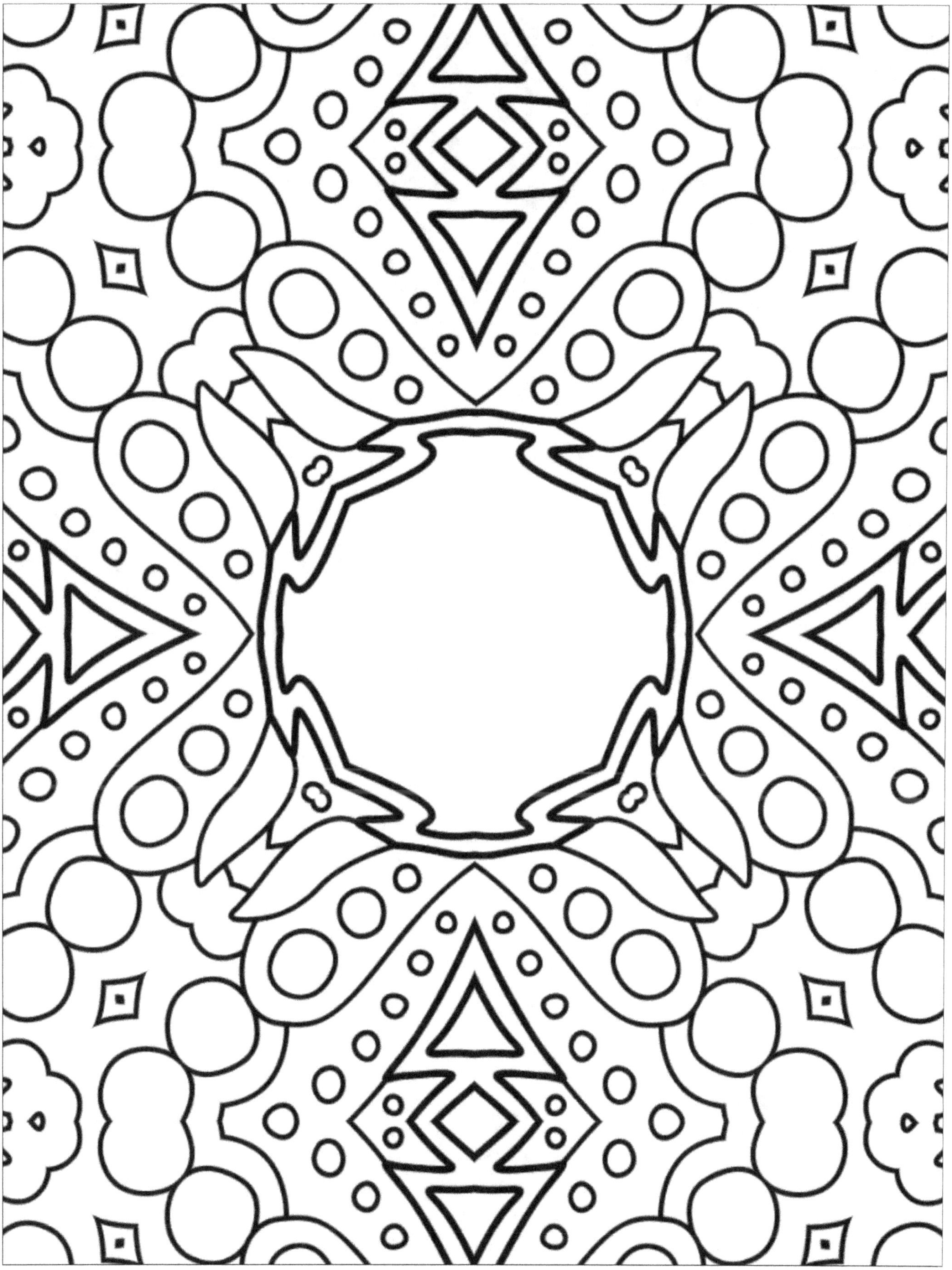

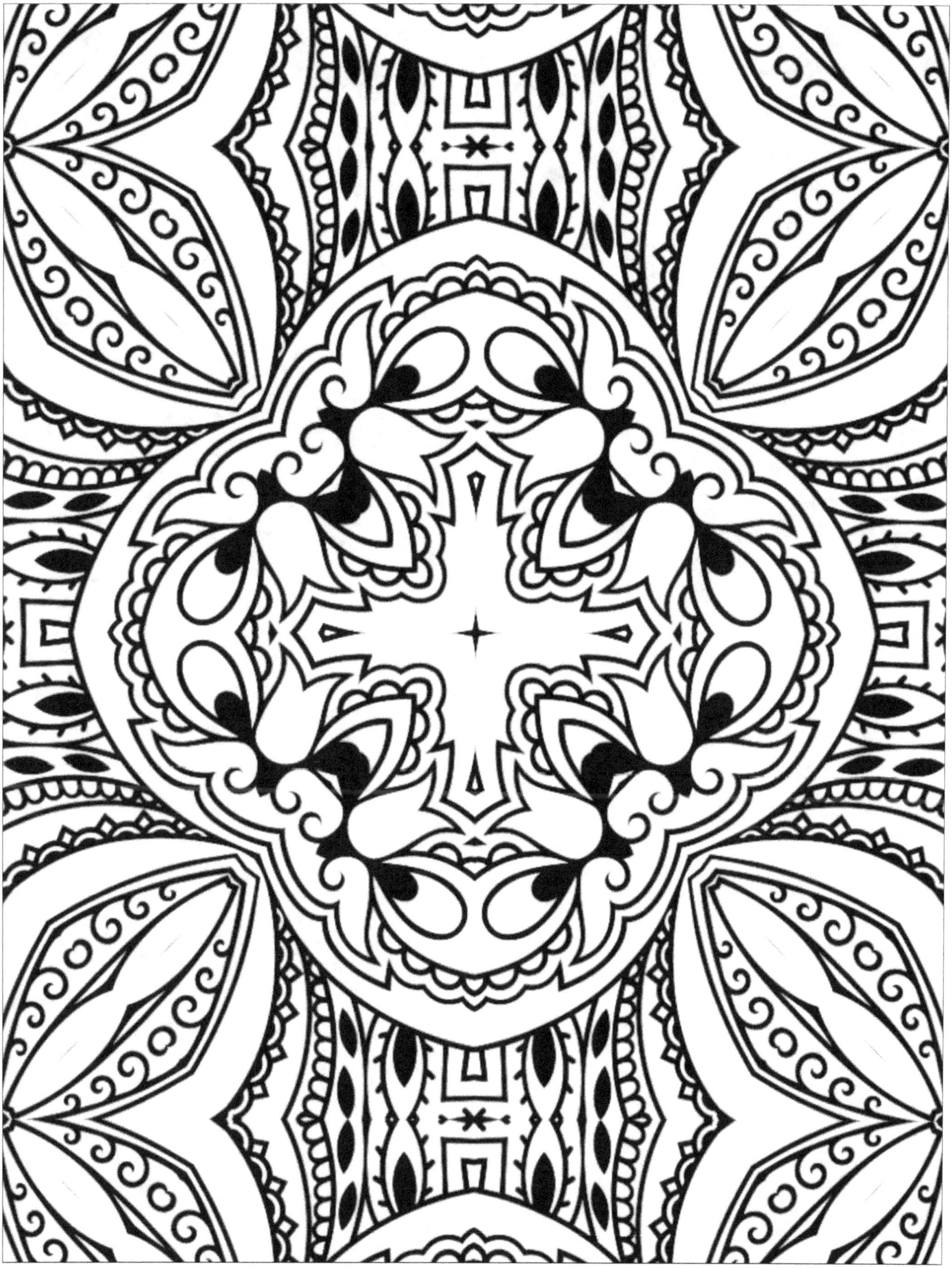

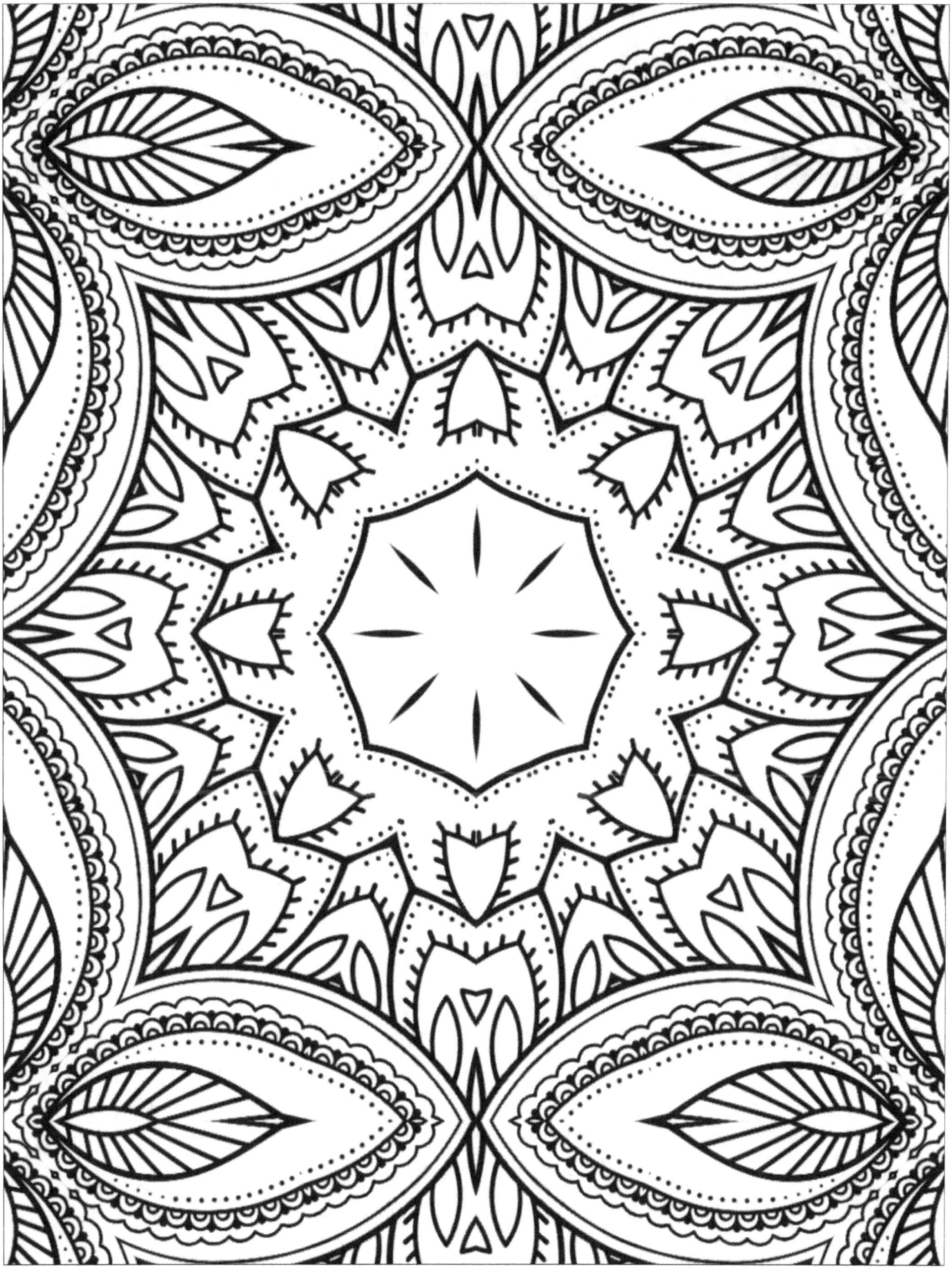

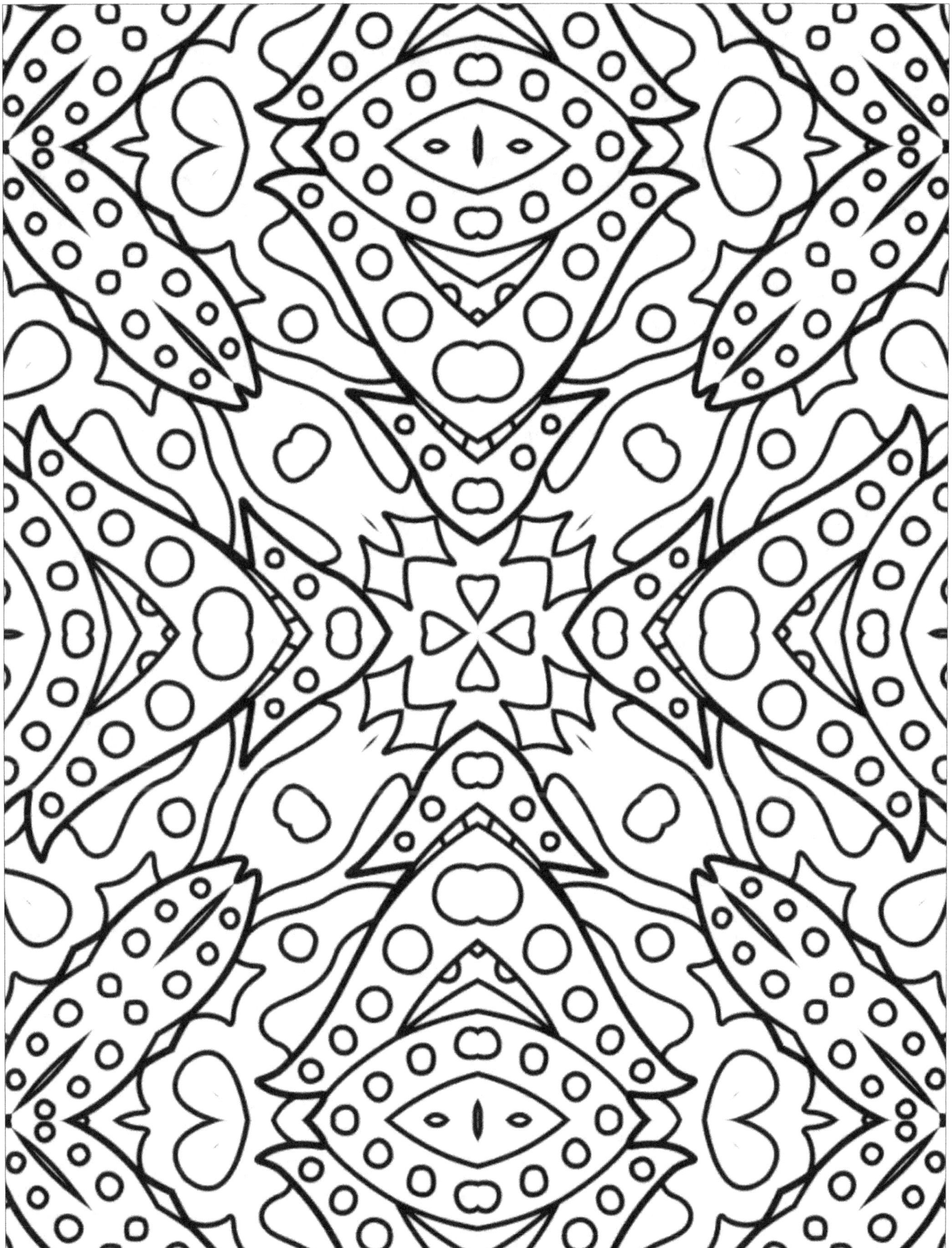

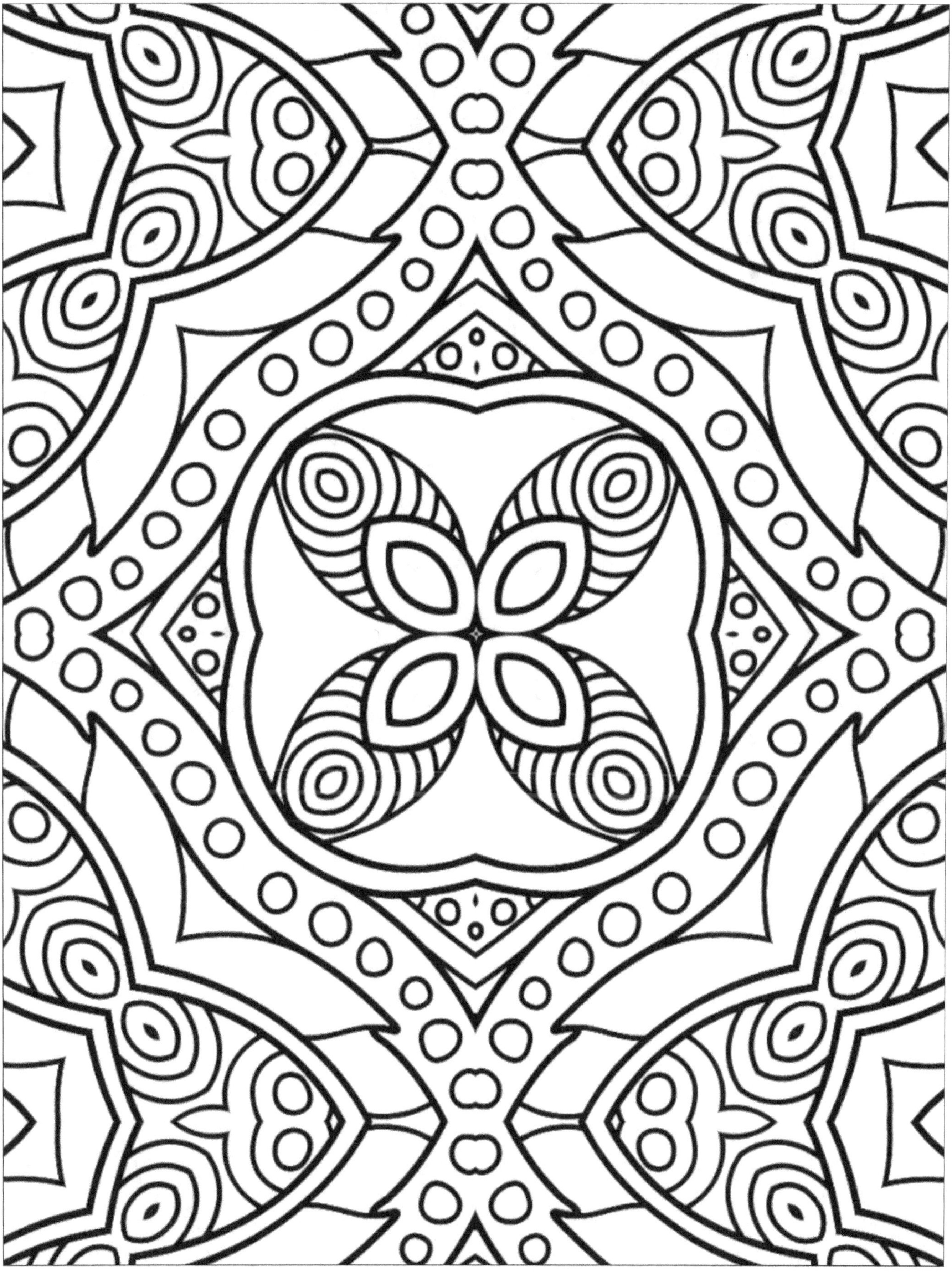

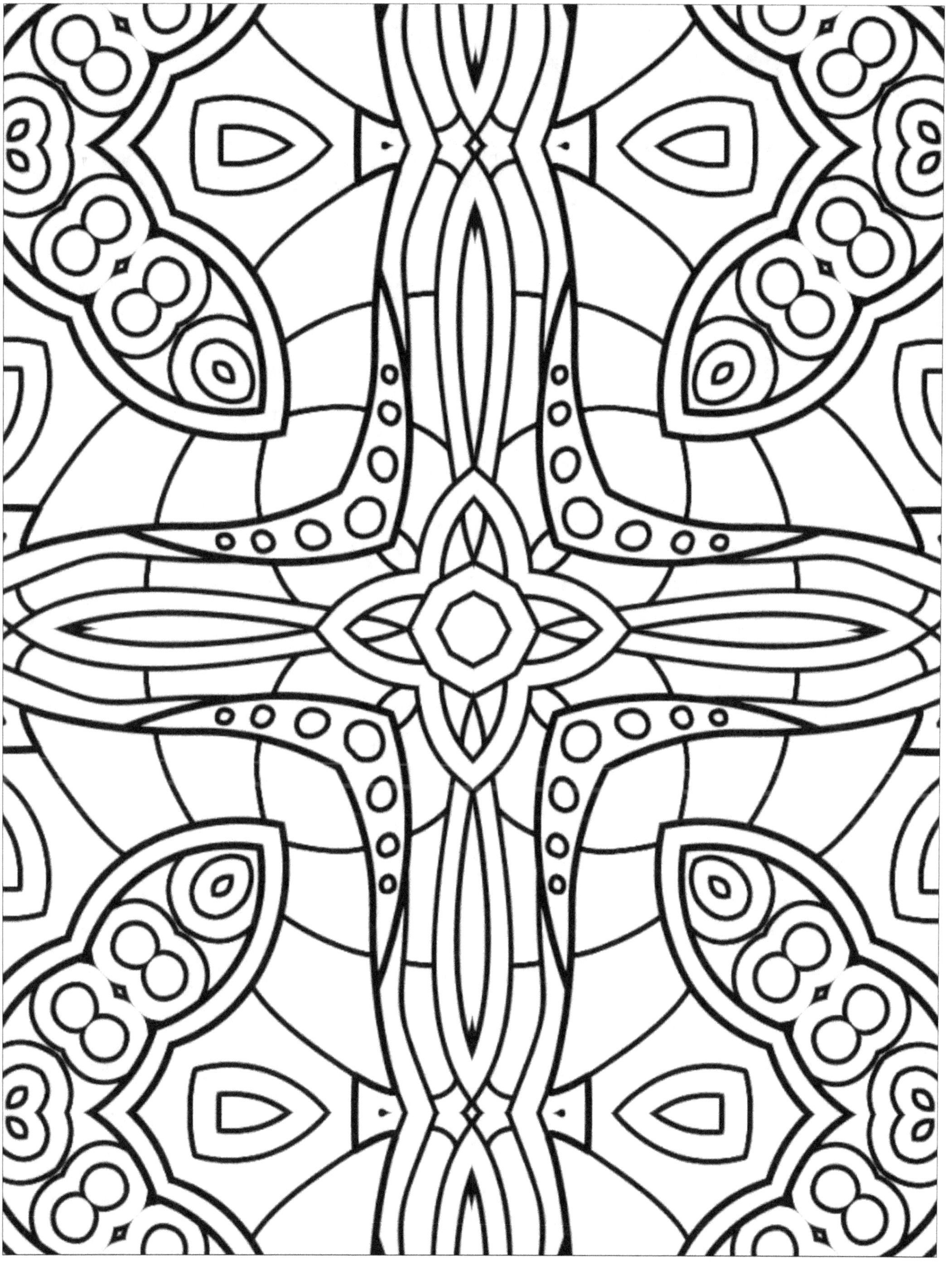

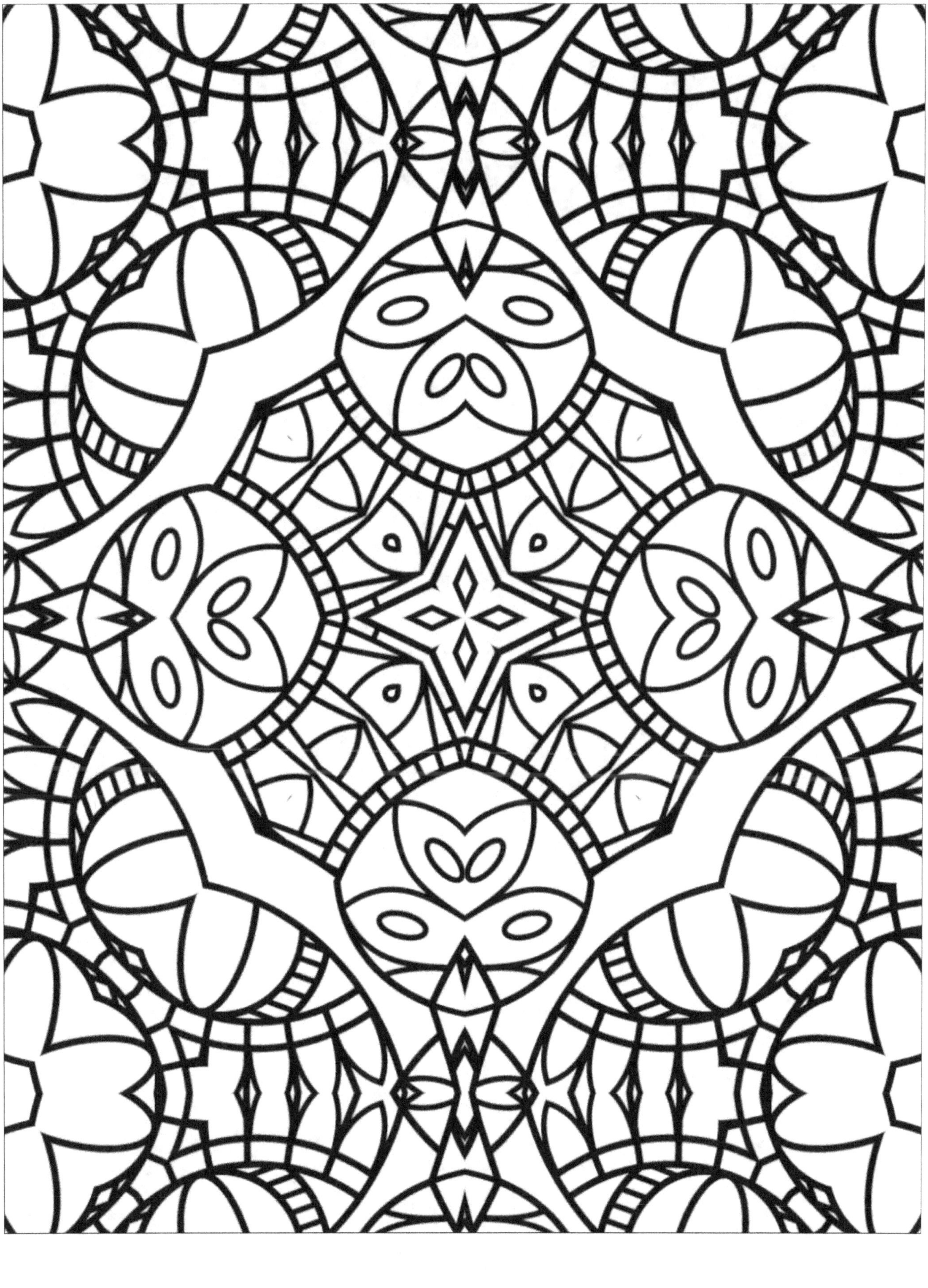

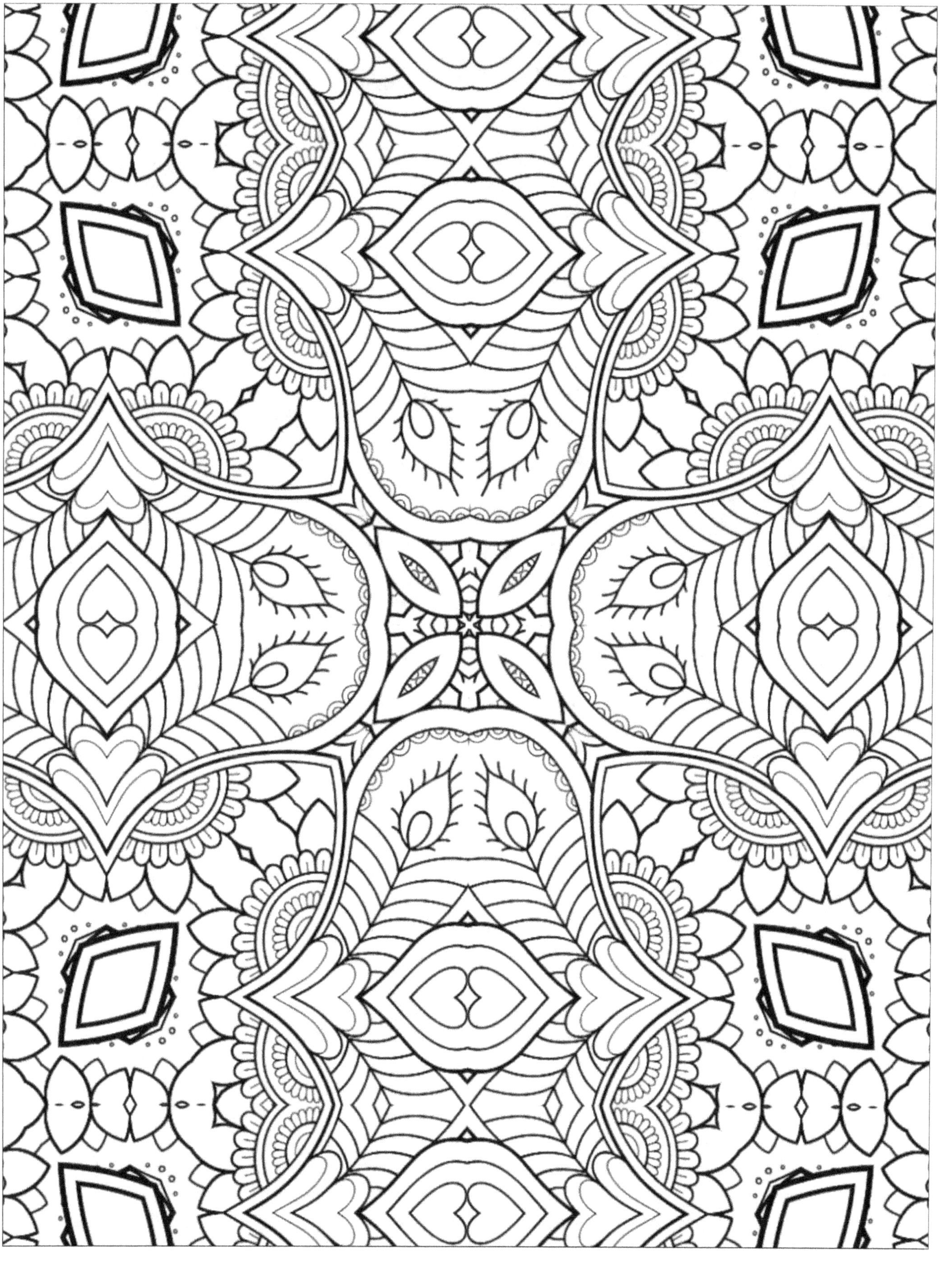

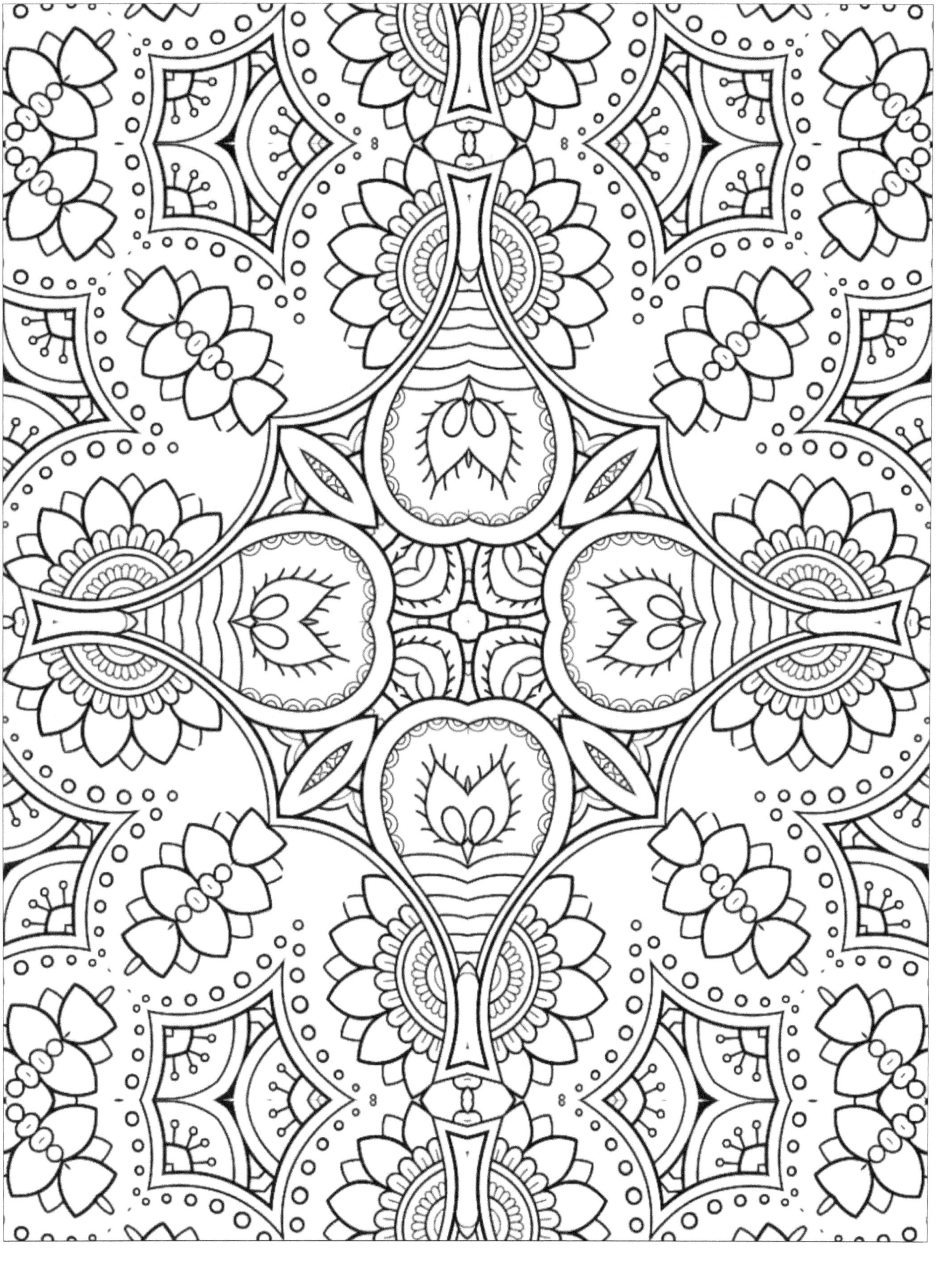

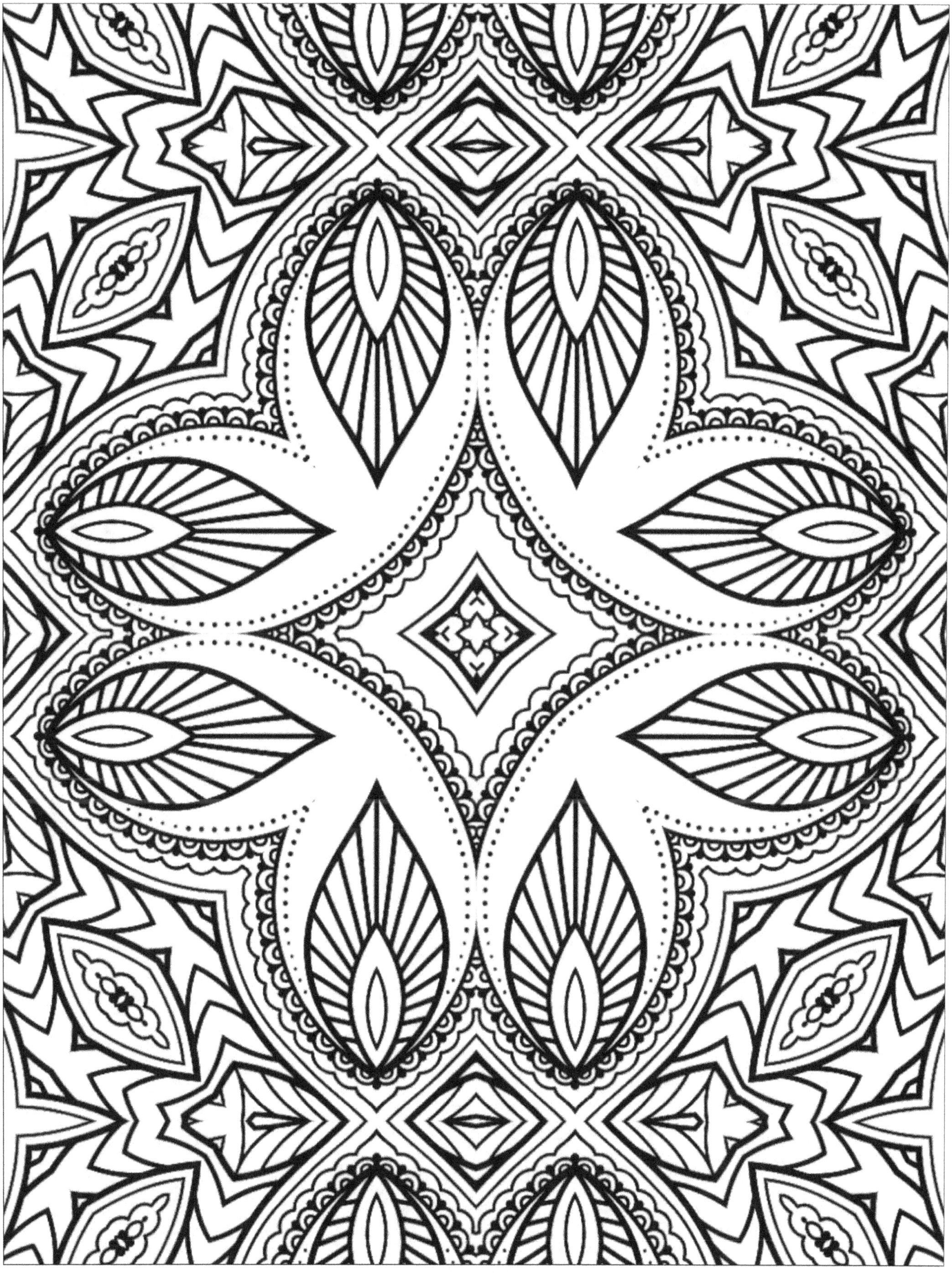

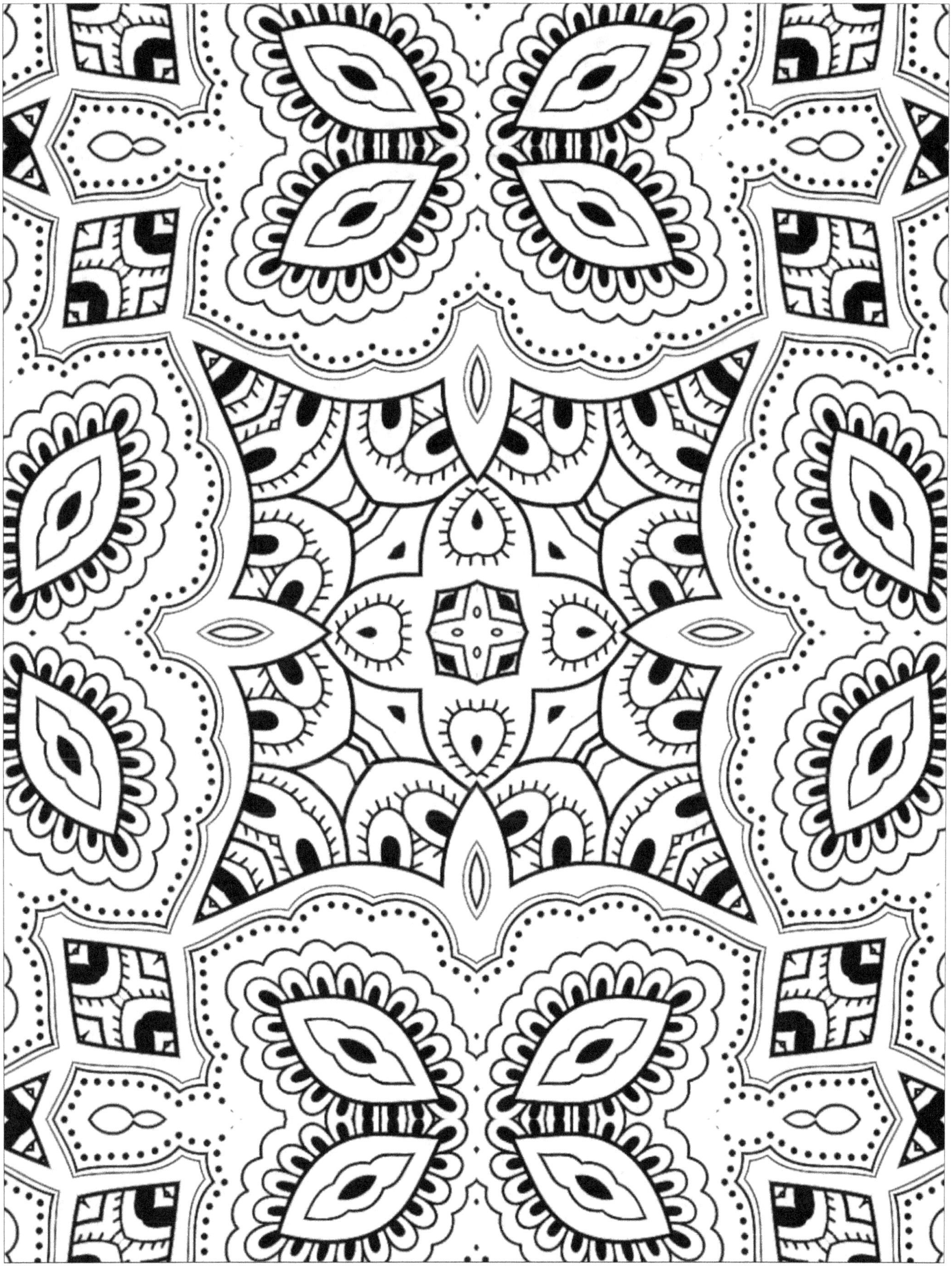

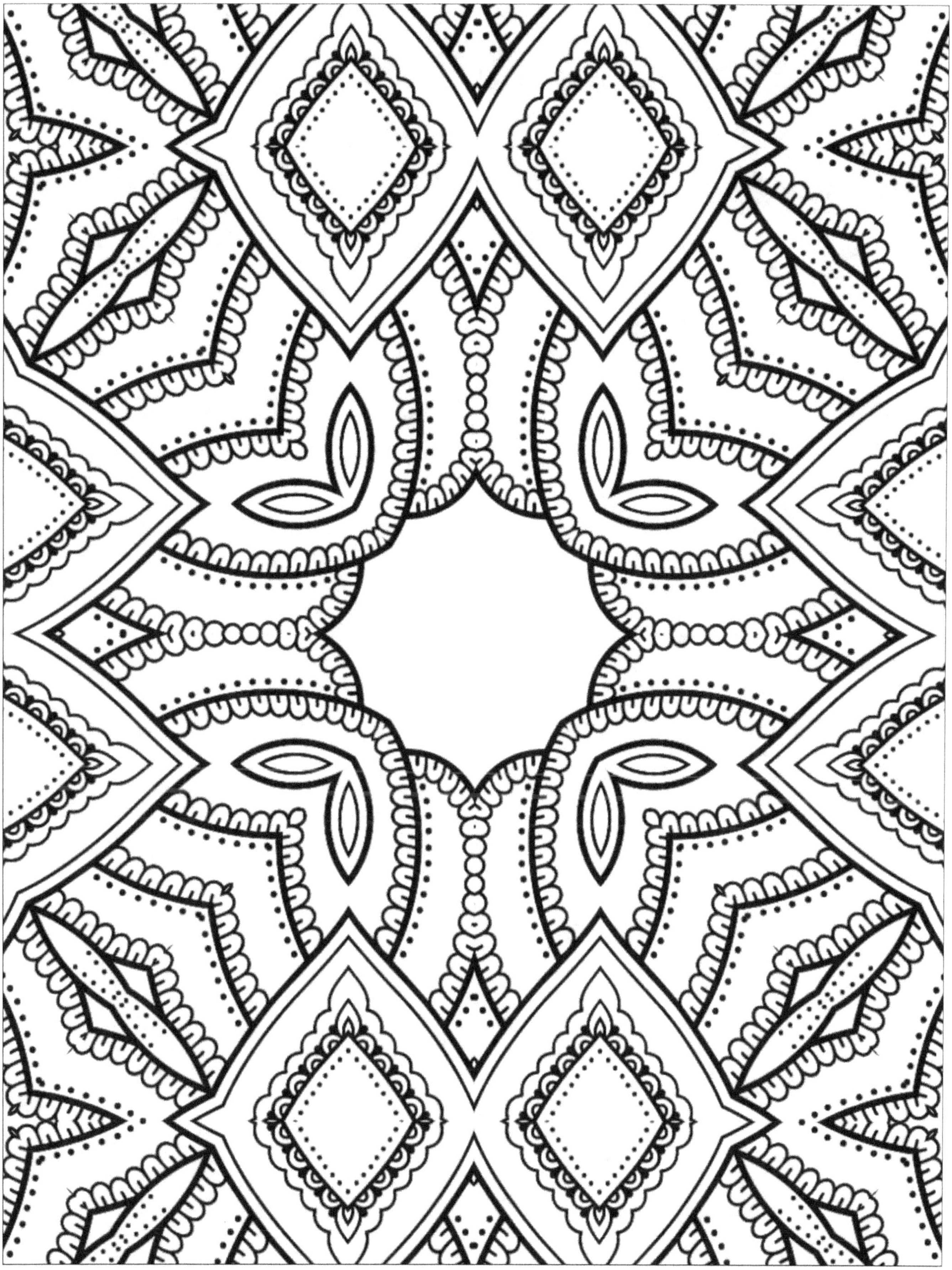

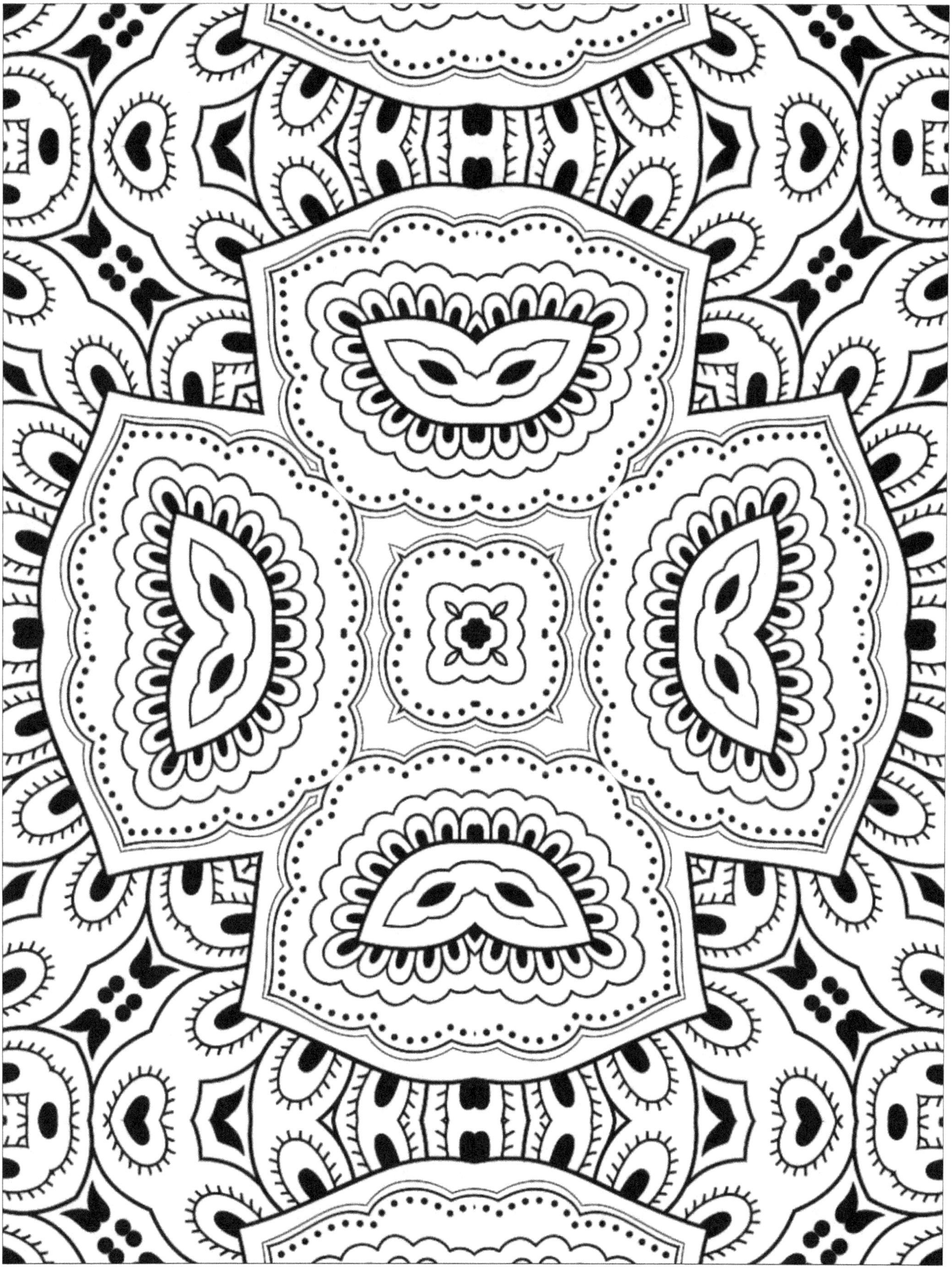

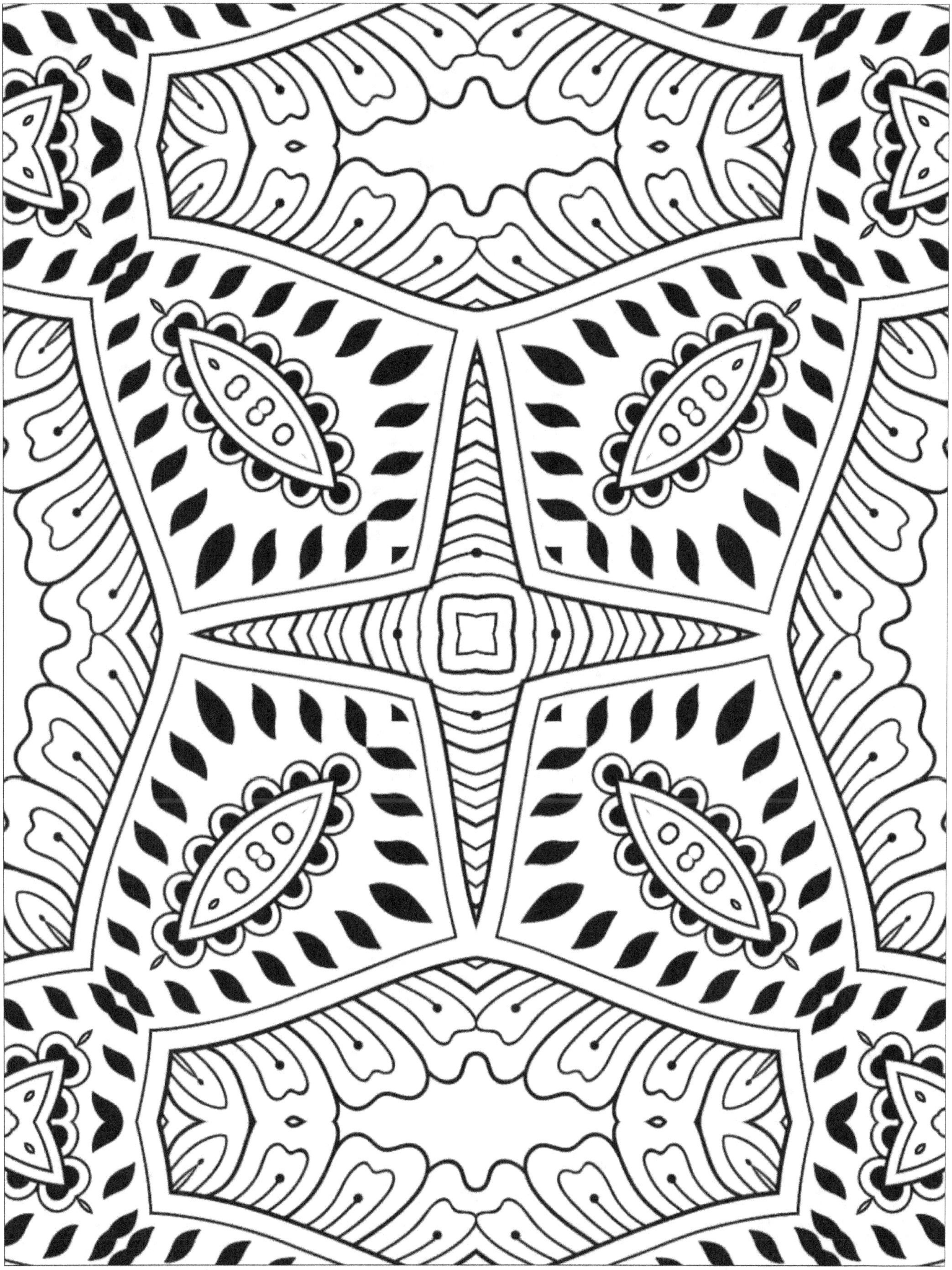

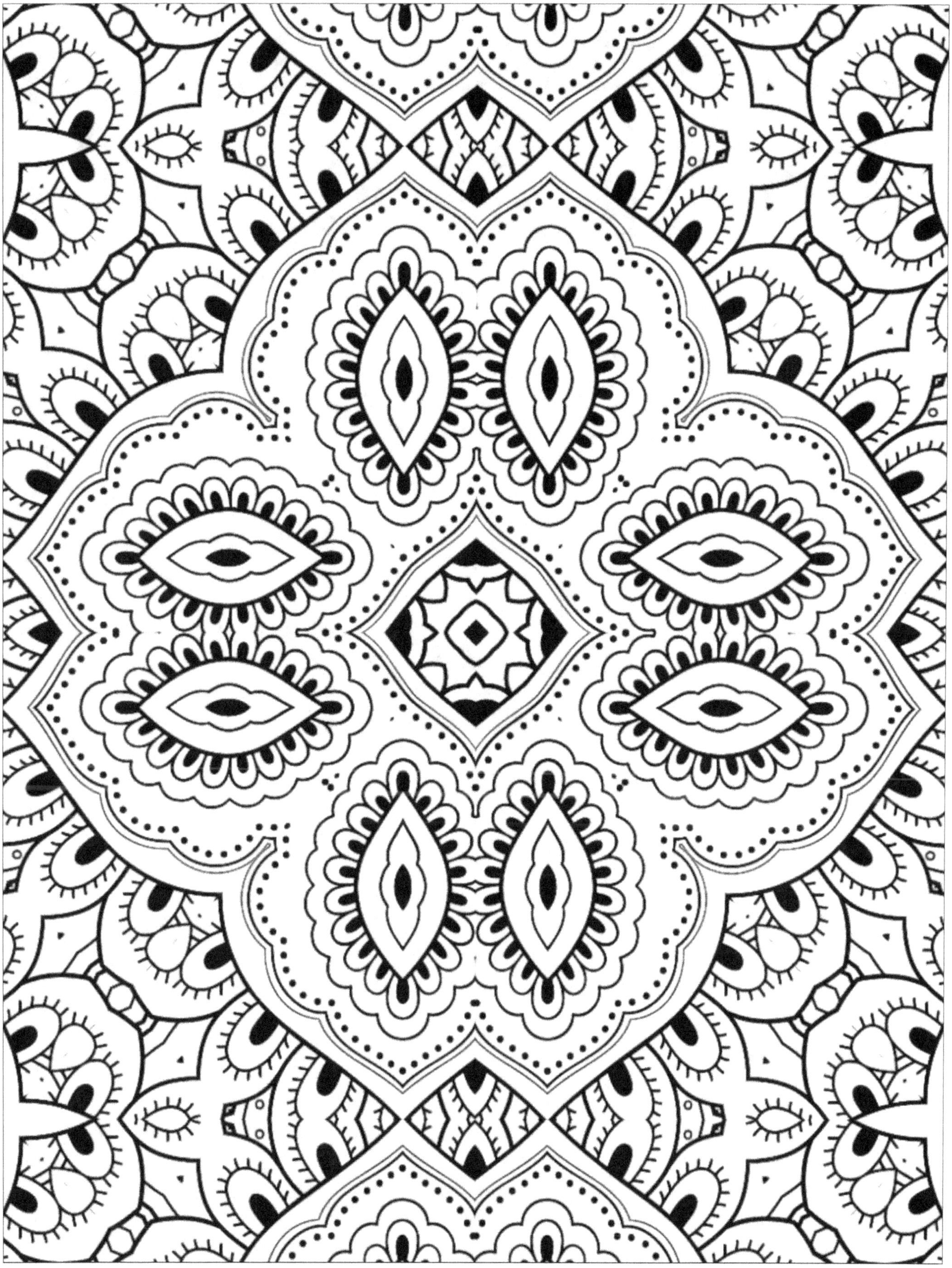

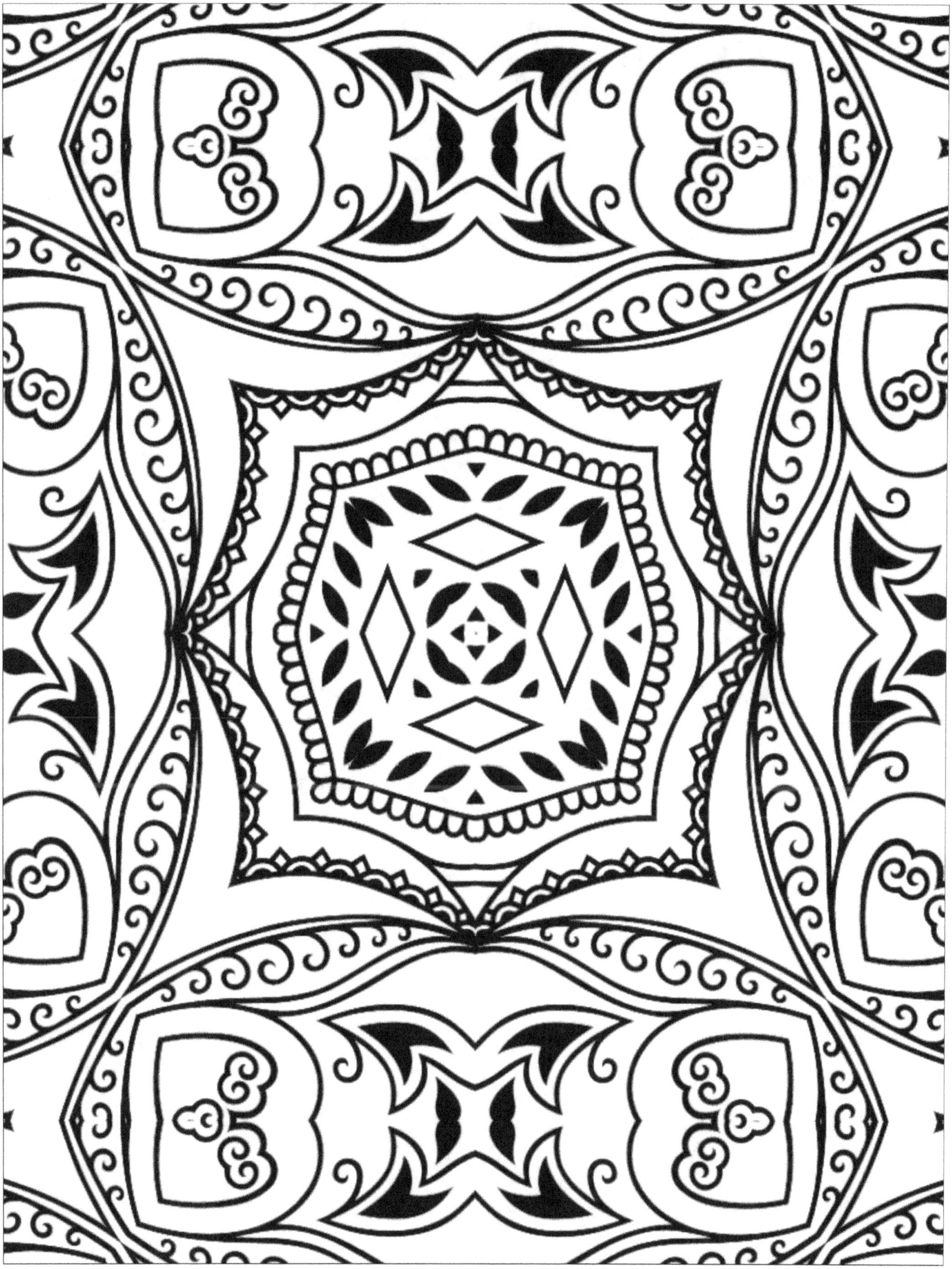

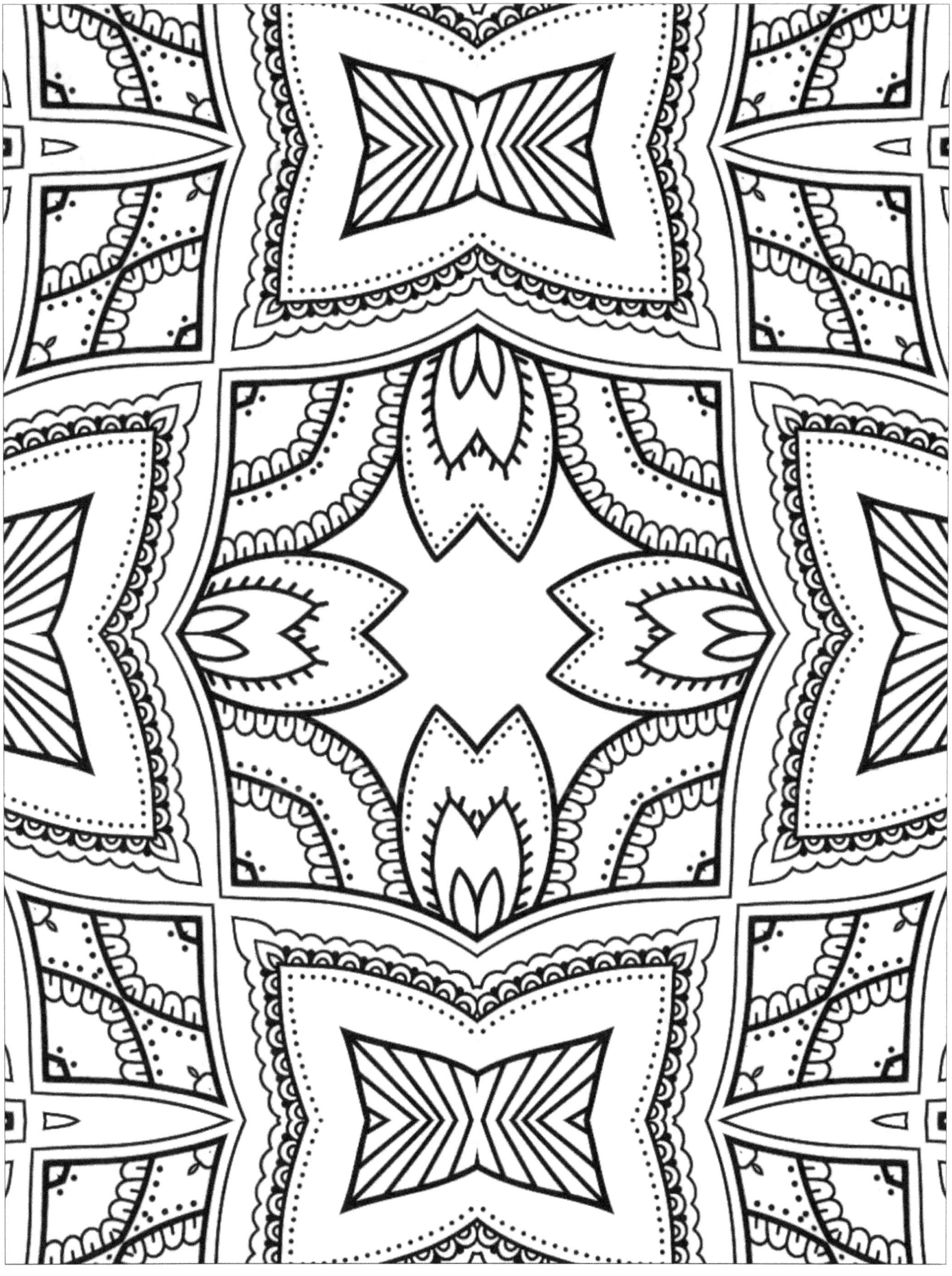

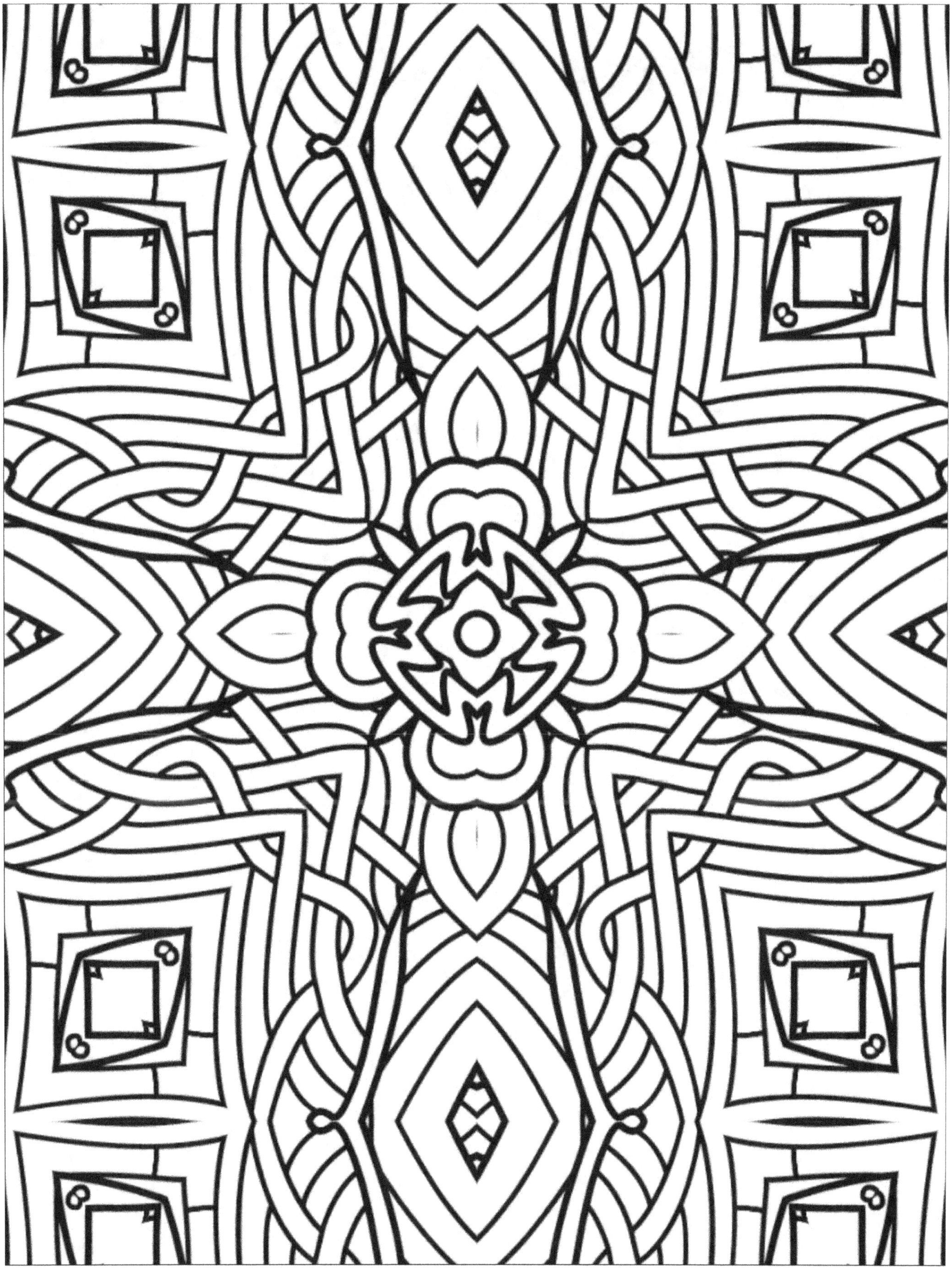

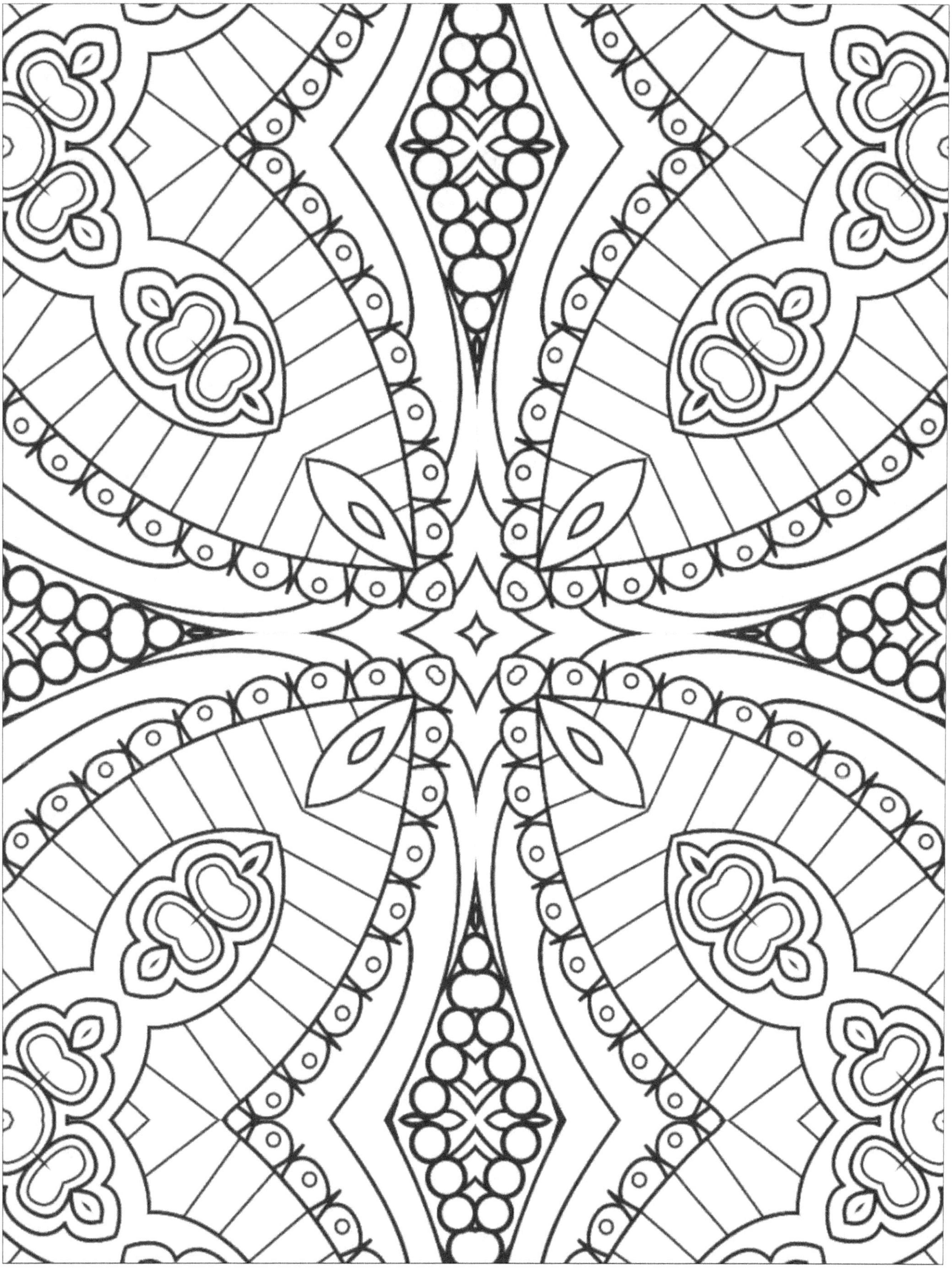

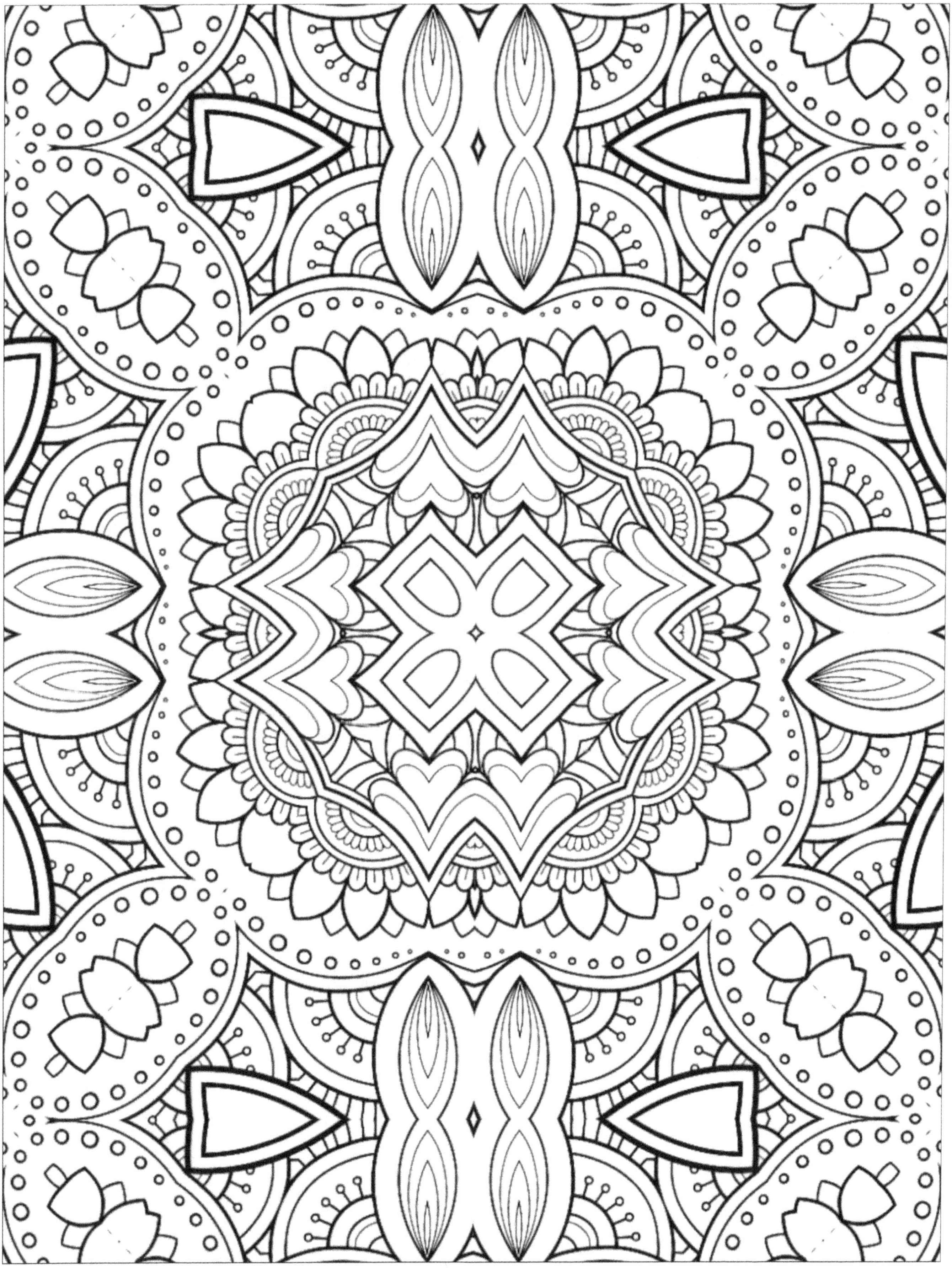

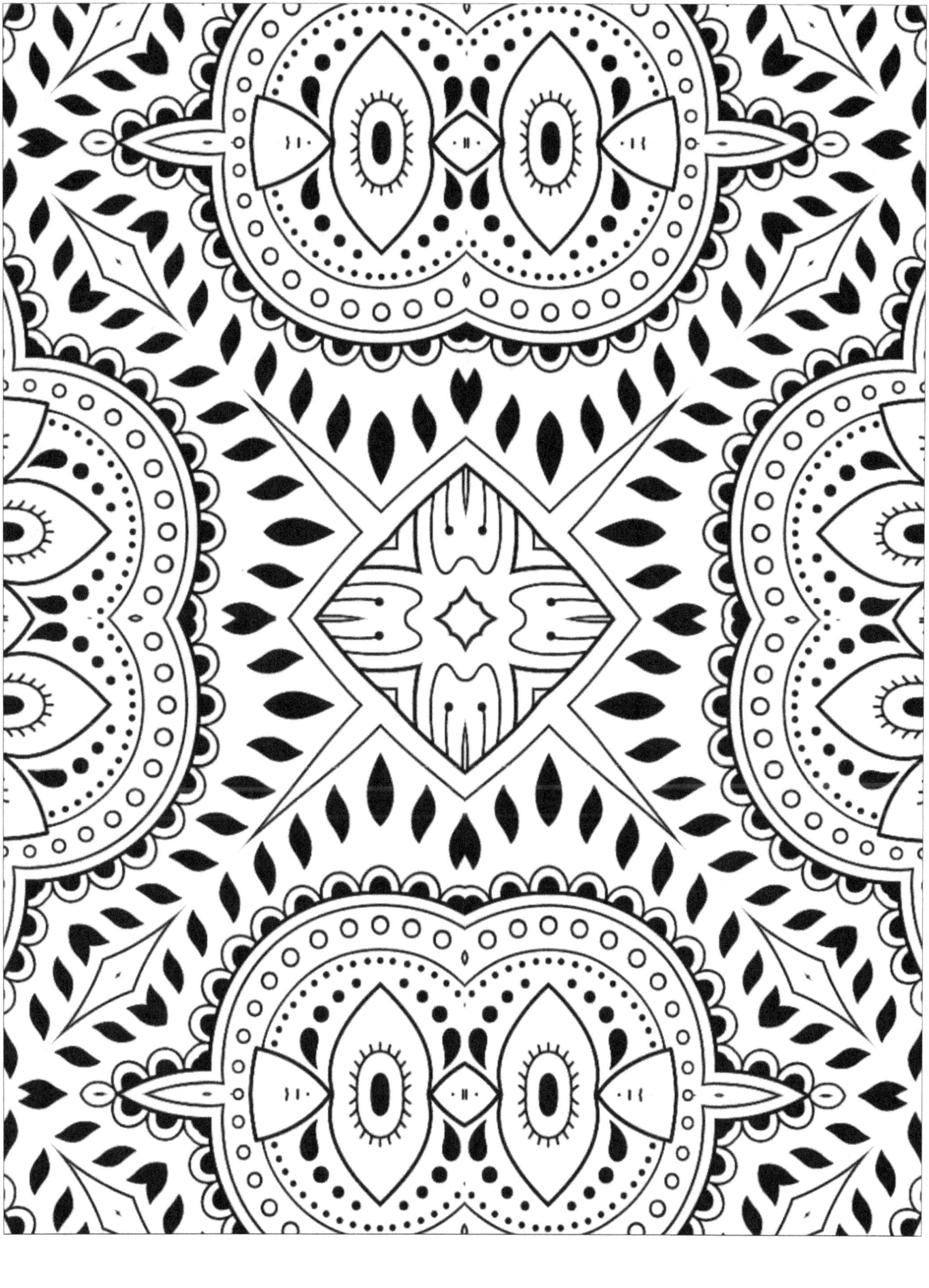

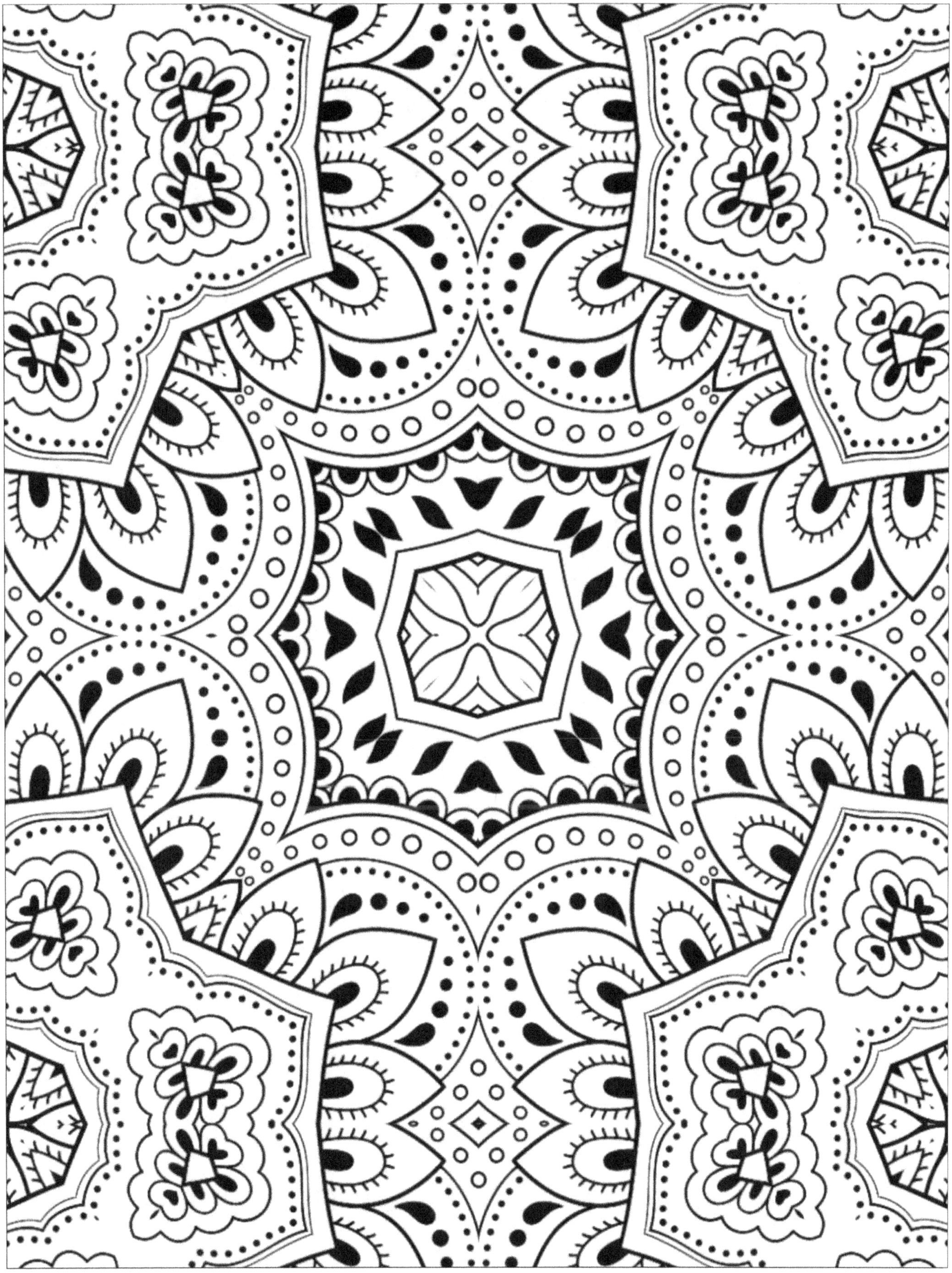

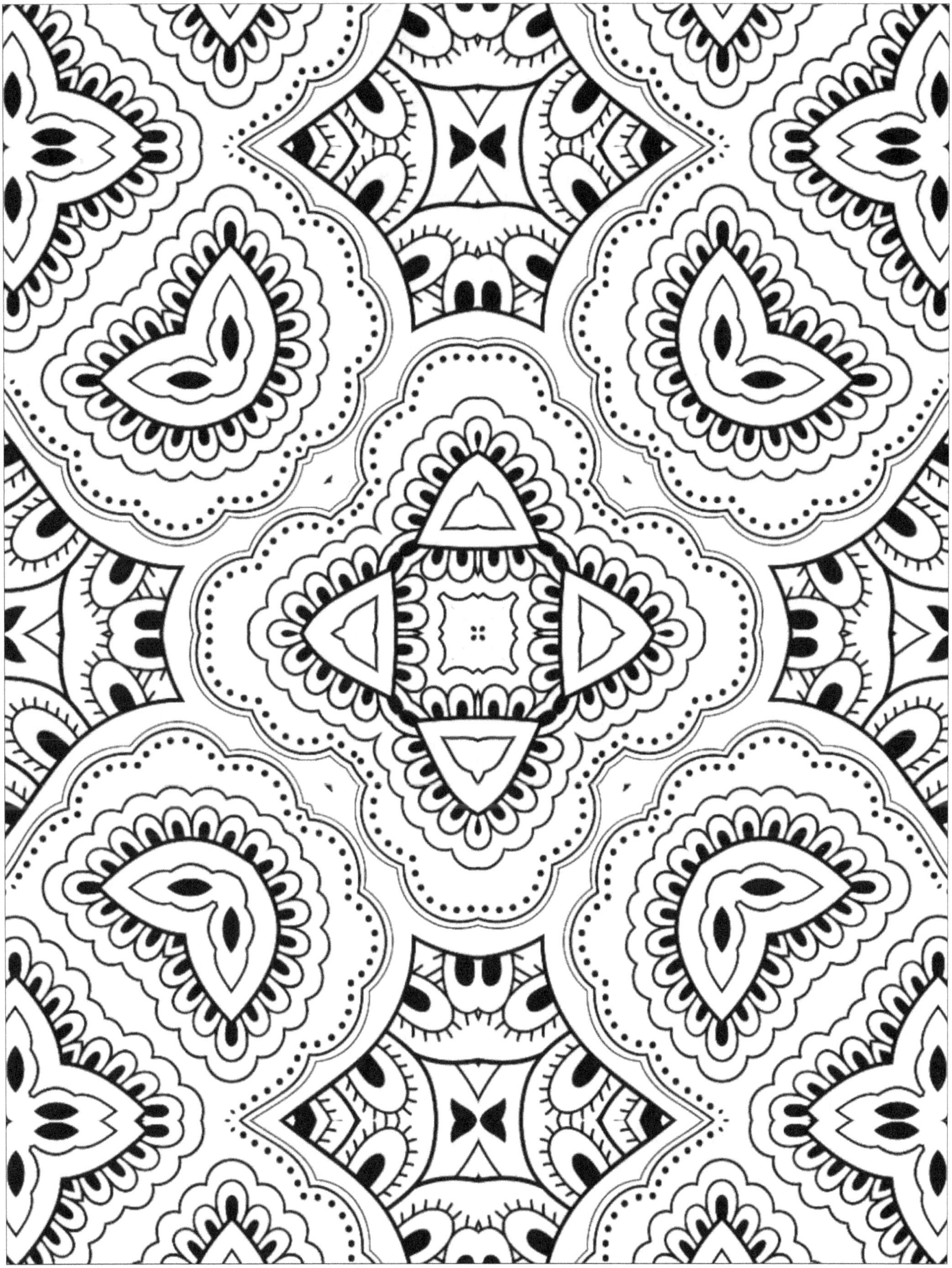

www.ingramcontent.com/pod-product-compliance
Lightning Source LLC
Chambersburg PA
CBHW081510220526
45467CB00010B/2851
9798700799775